WORD AND REDEEMER

THE AUTHORS

James M. Carmody, S.J., M.A., S.T.L., professor of theology at Le Moyne College, Syracuse, N.Y., is completing doctoral research at the Gregorian University, Rome. Thomas E. Clarke, S.J., S.T.L., S.T.D., who has taught dogmatic theology at Woodstock College, Woodstock, Md., since 1954, has also collaborated with Father Carmody on *Christ and His Mission: Christology and Soteriology* (Westminster, Md., Newman, 1966).

WORD AND REDEEMER

Christology in the Fathers

Prepared and Edited
with
Introduction and Commentary
by
JAMES M. CARMODY, S.J.
and
THOMAS E. CLARKE, S.J.

GUIDE TO THE FATHERS OF THE CHURCH

PAULIST PRESS GLEN ROCK, N.J.

Imprimi Potest: Edward J. Sponga, S.J.
Provincial, Maryland Prov.

September 30, 1965

Nihil Obstat: William F. Hogan
Censor Librorum

Imprimatur: Rt. Rev. James A. Hughes, V.G.
Archdiocese of Newark

January 7, 1966

Library of Congress
Catalog Card Number: 65-17864

COVER DESIGN: Claude Ponsot

Published by Paulist Press
Editorial Office: 304 W. 58th St., N. Y., N. Y. 10019
Business Office: Glen Rock, New Jersey 07452

Printed and bound in the
United States of America

ACKNOWLEDGMENTS

Unless credit is otherwise given, the translations are by the present authors. We express our thanks to the following for permission to use copyrighted material:

BRUCE PUBLISHING COMPANY, MILWAUKEE: *The Whole Christ,* by E. Mersch, tr. J. Kelly, 1938.

CATHOLIC UNIVERSITY OF AMERICA PRESS, WASHINGTON, D.C.: Fathers of the Church series: *Volume 2, Saint Augustine. Christian Instruction,* etc., 1947; *Volume 6, Saint Justin, Martyr,* tr. T. Falls, 1948; *Volume 20, Saint Augustine. Letters. Volume 2.* tr. W. Parsons, 1953; *Volume 23, Clement of Alexandria, Christ the Educator,* tr. S. Wood, 1954; *Volume 34, Saint Leo the Great. Letters,* tr. E. Hunt, 1957; *Volume 37, Saint John of Damascus. Writings,* tr. F. Chase, Jr., 1958.

HARVARD UNIVERSITY PRESS, CAMBRIDGE, MASS.: Loeb Classical Library: *Boethius. The Theological Tractates,* tr. H. Stewart & E. Rand, 1918; *Clement of Alexandria,* tr. G. Butterworth, 1919.

W. HEFFER & SONS, LTD., CAMBRIDGE, ENGLAND: *Commentary of Theodore of Mopsuestia on the Nicene Creed. Woodbrooke Studies. Volume 5,* 1932; *Commentary of Theodore of Mopsuestia on the Lord's Prayer and on the Sacraments of Baptism and the Eucharist. Woodbrooke Studies. Volume 6,* 1933. Ed. A. Mingana.

B. HERDER BOOK CO., ST. LOUIS AND LONDON: *The Church Teaches. Documents of the Church in English Translation,* tr. J. Clarkson et al., 1955.

METHUEN & CO., LTD., LONDON: *The Oecumenical Documents of the Faith,* 4th ed., ed. T. Bindley & F. Green, 1950.

OXFORD UNIVERSITY PRESS, NEW YORK AND LONDON: *Documents of the Christian Church,* ed. H. Bettenson, 1963; *The Early Christian Fathers,* ed. H. Bettenson, 1956.

RANDOM HOUSE, NEW YORK: *Basic Writings of Saint Augustine,* ed. W. Oates, Volume 1, 1948.

S.P.C.K., LONDON: *Selections from the Commentaries and Homilies of Origen,* tr. R. Tollinton, 1929; *Tertullian's Treatise against Praxeas,* ed. E. Evans, 1948; *Tertullian's Treatise on the Incarnation,* ed. E. Evans, 1956; *The Council of Chalcedon,* by R. Sellers. 1953.

WESTMINSTER PRESS, PHILADELPHIA: Library of Christian Classics. *Volume 2, Alexandrian Christianity,* ed. J. Oulton & H. Chadwick, 1954; *Volume 3, Christology of the Later Fathers,* ed. E. Hardy, 1954; *Volume 4, Cyril of Jerusalem and Nemesius of Emesa,* ed. W. Telfer, 1955.

CONTENTS

LIST OF ABBREVIATIONS

ACO	Acta Conciliorum Oecumenicorum, ed. E. Schwartz. Berlin, 1914ff.
ACW	Ancient Christian Writers, ed. J. Quasten et al. Westminster, Md., 1946ff.
Allies	Holy Images. London, 1898.
ANF	Ante-Nicene Fathers. Buffalo and New York.
Bettenson [1]	H. Bettenson, ed., Documents of the Christian Church. New York and London, 1963.
Bettenson [2]	H. Bettenson, ed., The Early Christian Fathers. New York and London, 1956.
BWA	Basic Writings of Saint Augustine, ed. W. Oates. New York, 1948.
CCL	Corpus Christianorum. Series Latina. Turnhout and Paris, 1953ff.
CSEL	Corpus Scriptorum Ecclesiasticorum Latinorum. Vienna, 1866ff.
DS	H. Denzinger and A. Schönmetzer, ed., Enchiridion Symbolorum Definitionum et Declarationum de Rebus Fidei et Morum. Freiburg, 1963.
Evans [1]	E. Evans, ed., Tertullian's Treatise on the Incarnation. London, 1956.
Evans [2]	E. Evans, ed., Tertullian's Treatise against Praxeas. London, 1948.
FC	The Fathers of the Church, ed. R. J. Deferrari. New York and Washington, 1947ff.
GCS	Die griechischen christlichen Schriftsteller. Leipzig, 1897ff.
LCC	Library of Christian Classics, ed. J. Baillie et al. Philadelphia and London, 1953ff.
LCL	Loeb Classical Library. London and Cambridge, Mass. 1912ff.
LFC	Library of the Fathers of the Holy Catholic Church, ed. E. Pusey et al. Oxford, 1838-88.
Mansi	J. D. Mansi, Sacrorum Conciliorum Nova et Amplissima Collectio.
Mersch	E. Mersch, The Whole Christ. Milwaukee, 1938.
NPNF	Nicene and Post-Nicene Fathers. New York.
ODF	The Oecumenical Documents of the Faith, ed. T. Bindley and F. Green. London, 1950.
PG	Migne, Patrologia Graeca.
PL	Migne, Patrologia Latina.
SC	Scuola Cattolica. Milan, 1873ff.
Sellers	R. Sellers, The Council of Chalcedon. London, 1953.
TCT	The Church Teaches, ed. J. Clarkson et al. St. Louis, 1955.
Tollinton	R. Tollinton, tr., Selections from the Commentaries and Homilies of Origen. London, 1929.
WS	Woodbrooke Studies. Manchester.
Xiberta	B. Xiberta, ed., Enchiridion de Verbo Incarnato. Madrid, 1957.
Note:	Scriptural abbreviations used in the Guide series generally follow the KJV-RSV tradition.

GENERAL INTRODUCTION

What do the fathers say of Christ? Before we get on to their writings about Christology—their Christ-theology—we should know a bit about their intellectual interests and their style of learned conversation. On both counts they stand as a kind of bridge somewhere between the New Testament writers who precede them and the medieval theologians who come afterward.

The New Testament writers have a functional theology. They think concretely and write narratives in which the significance of a person is seen in what he does, in the story and history of what happens. They are rarely if ever concerned with abstract philosophical questions. Their direct concern is with what Christ is *for us,* what role he fulfills in the history of salvation. They do not worry about what he is in his inmost being: they are not concerned with metaphysics or ontology. The medieval theologian, on the other hand, is deeply concerned with metaphysical questions—with the problems of essence and existence, nature and person, substance and accident, intellect and will. He is a scholastic—i.e., he studies and writes within a medieval school environment where philosophical speculation abounds and abstraction is a way of life.

The fathers, as we said above, stand as a kind of bridge between the theology of the New Testament and that of the middle ages. The beginnings of patristic theology may be sketched roughly as follows. As the gospel moves from the Semitic to the Hellenistic world, from the Jew to the Greek, there is a shift in what Christians think about and the way they express themselves. The Greek mind (in this a noble representative of the human spirit) raises questions which cannot be adequately answered in functional language. The Greek mind asks not only "What is Christ *for me*?" but "Who is he *in himself*?" Is he God or creature or both? And if both, how are we to conceive the relation between the divine and the human in him? Are they identical or distinct or both? And if both, how do we explain this?

Such questions may be less gripping and graspable for the religious imagination than questions about whether and how man has been truly rescued from the absurdities of human existence. But the questions of the Greek mind are, nonetheless, questions which the human mind cannot avoid if it is to be true to itself. And these questions must be properly answered if man is ever to get valid answers to the other, more immediate questions about the human condition.

The Church of the fathers faced these questions under pressures that were not only doctrinal, but also pastoral, political, and cultural. The fathers could not live in an ivory tower. For example, heresy to them was not merely an intellectual deviation, but a terrible, frightening moral and religious specter. Heresy meant schism, meant wounding the body of Christ, meant threatening the life of God's people and betraying the savior and the inspired word of God in scripture. The Church then was acutely aware of the meaning of orthodoxy—i.e., right Christian doctrine—and heterodoxy—i.e., doctrine alien to Christianity. This burning concern for rightness of teaching accounts in large part for the vehement and sometimes violent tone of patristic polemics; it accounts too for the political ruses and physical force sometimes employed in defense of the faith. On some occasions monks emerged from their cloisters and lay people from their homes to take up cudgels in the struggle for the triumph of one dogmatic position or another. If we have learned in modern times to see the difference between truth and our own frail grasp of it, we may, nevertheless, have lost something of the early Church's passionate dedication to the truth itself. We may also have lost the keen realization of those times that today's deviation in thought may be tomorrow's religious and moral apostasy.

Such was the atmosphere in which the fathers confronted the Christological questions of their age. And as the special kinds of questions raised by Greek philosophy were put forward, the more scriptural questions, the questions about soteriology (about Christ as savior, and savior "for me"), began to recede. But it would be a grave mistake to think that soteriology was of no concern to the patristic period. Scripture and salvation continued to be normative, to be the touchstones. Any metaphysical teaching which left man or any part of him unredeemed was anathema as far as the fathers were concerned. We will return to this subject shortly. For the present, we can take note of the fact that the fathers are moving away from the scriptural viewpoint toward the medieval viewpoint: they are leaving an age in which Christology was imbedded in soteriology, and moving toward a time when soteriology is imbedded in Christology.

In the following pages we will be mainly concerned with four general themes, listed here in the order in which they dominated the fathers' thinking about Christ.

A. The Basic Christological Problem: the One-and-Many in Christ

The Council of Chalcedon in 451 gave a decisive answer to this problem. Chalcedon proclaimed that one and the same Jesus Christ, the eternal Son of God, the son of Mary, is true and perfect God, true and perfect man, a single hypostasis or person in two distinct natures. This formula, however, was the result of long development and the basis of later development. It will help if we trace here the general lines of these developments, seeking both logical clarity and historical accuracy.

The mystery of Christ, Karl Adam has written, is not that he is God, but that he is the God-man (*The Son of God*: New York, 1940, p. 1). The Christological problem in the strict sense is concerned with the relationship of the humanity and divinity truly co-present in the savior. So it arises only when the co-presence of genuine humanity and divinity has been established. This is obvious logically; but it is also by and large true of what happened historically. The strict Christological problem arose in acute form only in the late fourth century, when the true and integral humanity and the perfect divinity of Christ had finally been clearly affirmed. Let us trace the development in a brief and somewhat abstract outline:

1. HUMANITY

(a) *The body:* The first truth about Christ to be challenged and defended was his humanity and particularly his bodily reality. From the beginning gnostic dualism, wishing to keep God as pure spirit from direct contact with the impurities of matter, denied the reality of the human body, birth, suffering and death of the savior. This was the heresy of *docetism* (Gk: *dokein,* to seem, appear). And from Ignatius of Antioch on, the Church vigorously asserted that Christ had a true body of flesh, truly born from Mary, and that he truly suffered and died.

(b) *The soul:* The attack on the human mind of Christ came in the fourth century, from (as we shall see) Arianism and especially Apollinarianism. Both thought that the Word (for Arians a creature, for Apollinarians true God) took the place of a human mind in the savior. Both of these views followed the Word-flesh schema, which we shall see shortly. The first Council of Constantinople in 381 met this error in its condemnation of Apollinarianism.

2. DIVINITY

The divinity of Christ had also been questioned or compromised from early days. The Ebionites, a Judaeo-Christian sect, considered Jesus to be a mere man with a special relationship to God. Various forms of adoptionism (seeing Jesus as God's "adopted son") sprang up in the first few centuries. But the main challenge to the divinity of Christ came from Arius, who considered the Son to be the most perfect of creatures, subordinate to the Father-Creator. The Council of Nicaea (325) defined in its creed the equal divinity of the Son with the Father. Several decades of the fourth century after Nicaea were required to confirm and clarify the Nicene dogma. This fascinating story is material for a whole volume in itself; the present study will only incidentally touch on the Nicene crisis and the precise question of the divinity of Christ.

And so by 381, the orthodox patristic portrait of Christ was as follows: He is truly man, with a body subject to death (against docetism), and a human mind or spiritual soul (against Arianism and Apollinarianism). He is truly and perfectly God, equal to and distinct from the Father (against Arianism). Now, finally, the time is ripe for the Christological question in the strict sense, the question of the relationship of humanity and divinity, to take the center of the stage. Logically, two sets of answers are possible. Historically, these two possibilities took the form of two Christologies: the Word-flesh (roughly, Alexandrian) Christology, and the Word-man (Antiochene) Christology.

(a) *The Word-flesh Christology of Alexandria:* This view stressed the unity of Christ, the fact that it is one and the same who is both God and man. It ran the risk, however, of lessening the reality and completeness of his humanity. Its characteristic formula was the Joannine "The Word was made flesh" (Jn 1:14). It insisted that the Word took to himself and made his own the flesh drawn from Mary. Largely through stoic influence, it tended to make the divine Word (*logos* or reason) preempt in Christ the place of his human *logos* or mind. In its moderate form (Athanasius, Cyril of Alexandria), it did not deny the presence of a human mind in the savior, but Athanasius, and, to a lesser extent Cyril, failed to give the human mind and will of Christ an active role in our salvation. In its extreme form, the Word-flesh Christology led Arianism and Apollinarism to deny the need and possibility of a human mind in Christ; the divine Word assumed this function. For them, too, as for Dioscorus, Eutyches and the monophysites (who said Christ has only one nature), divinity and humanity formed not only a single person but a single nature. The Word-flesh Christology, as defended by Cyril, triumphed at Ephesus (431) in the condemnation of Nestorius (see below). Twenty years later, however, monophysitism was condemned by Chalcedon (451).

(b) *The Word-man Christology of Antioch:* This approach stressed the reality and integrality of both natures in Christ. It did so out of concern for the divine transcendence of the Word, who must not, it was felt, become enmeshed in the weaknesses of the flesh; and there was also concern for the synoptic gospels' portrayal of Jesus as fully a man. Antioch's characteristic formula spoke of the "Man assumed" (*Homo assumptus*) by the Word. The son of Mary is spoken of as distinct from the Word, and assumed by or united to him in a perfect union. In its extreme form (Nestorianism), this view refused to attribute the actions and sufferings of Jesus to the Word of God, and denied that Mary was genuinely the *theotokos* (mother of God), insisting she was only the mother of Christ. There is a good deal of discussion today as to whether the leading representatives of this view, Theodore of Mopsuestia and Nestorius, were really heretical in their thought. John of Antioch is a good example of the moderate Antiochene view. Nestorianism met defeat at Ephesus, as we have said. But in 433 Cyril and John of Antioch agreed on a *Formula of Union*. Antioch also made a prominent contribution to the definition of Chalcedon (451), which rejected both extremes by defining that Christ is one hypostasis, one person, in two abidingly distinct natures. We may note also that the Christology of the West, mainly a Word-man Christology, also contributed to the definition of 451, particularly through Pope Leo's *Tome to Flavian*. With these two ecumenical councils, we are at the peak of the great Christological debate and its resolution.

Cyril's more radical followers would not accept Chalcedon, and there resulted an unfortunate schism of the monophysite churches of Egypt and Syria. Many scholars today feel that their monophysitism was more verbal than real. The next few centuries witnessed two major but unsuccessful efforts to reconcile them. The first of these attempts, under Emperor Justinian, culminated in the Second Council of Constantinople (551), which condemned the writings of Theodore and of two other Antiochenes of the previous century. The other effort took the form of a willingness on the part of some, encouraged by Pope Honorius, to deny that there are two wills and two kinds of activity in the God-man. The Third Council of Constantinople (681) ended this threat of monothelitism (the heresy that Christ has only one will). The import of this council was that it applied the Chalcedonian solution (one person and two natures) to the sphere of volition and action (one person but two wills and two levels of action). But Chalcedon remains the decisive early council even to our own day.

B. The Soteriological Argument in the Christological Disputes

The second theme which will occur frequently is the soteriological concern of the fathers. It is important to stress this today, when there is a tendency to set the Christological (ontological), and the soteriological (functional), i.e., what Christ was and what he did, in sharp opposition to each other. Scholastic theology of recent centuries has, unfortunately, too much separated the two. Harnack's charge that the gospel was hellenized by the fathers, while now commonly rejected, still finds more subtle echoes. And the ontological preoccupations of Nicaea and Chalcedon are often looked upon as regrettable, even if necessary, displacements of Christian focus. We will try to show by a sampling of patristic texts that, while the conciliar definitions and the immediate issues at stake were Christological, the underlying concern was soteriological. Against docetism, Arianism, Apollinarianism, Nestorianism, monophysitism, monothelitism, the same soteriological principle constantly recurs: *What was not assumed* (i.e., whatever in humanity was not united in Christ with the divine person of the Word) *was not healed*. Each of these heresies was seen not merely as falsifying the constitution of Christ but as threatening our salvation by Christ. The fathers, especially the Greek fathers, began from the so-called *physico-mystical* conception of the redemption: in the incarnation there occurred a *physical union* between the Word and a single human nature, which somehow *mystically contained* all men. Thus the presence and the action of the Word in this humanity, which is *our* humanity, is of itself a presence and action which saves humanity. This view drew on the scriptural doctrine of our solidarity with Christ (e.g., Heb 2:11); it also drew on Platonic ideas about the unity of mankind. It was and remains a rich and attractive link between Christology and soteriology.

C. Aspects of Redemption

Since the primary area of controversy and development was Christological, not soteriological, we find in the fathers little in the way of systematic soteriology. But as we read the texts, it will be interesting to note the different ways the fathers view salvation, by analogy with more or less familiar human relationships, situations, and realities. We may here briefly classify these principal aspects of redemption: (1) *illumination* by the law, teaching and example of the revealing Word incarnate; (2) *victory* of Christ over Satan, sin and death; (3) *liberation* (redemption, salvation) of man from the power of Satan, sin and death; (4) *ransom* paid in the blood of Christ (to the Father or to Satan); (5) *expiatory sacrifice* offered by Christ on our behalf; (6) *mediation* reconciling us with the Father in a new covenant; (7) *physico-mystical solidarity* (explained above).

D. Consequences of the Christological One-and-Many

Implicit in the truth of the incarnation are certain consequences, touching either the *human endowments* of the savior or the *proper way of speaking* of him. As to human endowments, we will encounter especially statements about the sinlessness of Christ, and the extent and limitations of his knowledge. As to the proper way of speaking about Christ, we will see again and again the so-called *mutual predication of properties* (technically, *communicatio idiomatum,* "communication of idioms"). It may be well to explain this here, because of its importance and frequency. Because it is one and the same person in Christ who exists in and acts through both human and divine natures, I may legitimately predicate of this one person both human (e.g., suffering) and divine (e.g., omnipotence) attributes. But more than this: I may predicate of the one concrete Christ, even when I name him according to his humanity, attributes which he has not in virtue of his humanity but in virtue of his divinity. This is also true in the opposite direction. Thus I may say: Mary's son is omnipotent; or: the eternal Word was born from Mary.

Here I am neither attributing omnipotence to human nature (which I would be doing if I said: Christ's humanity is omnipotent), nor attributing human birth to divinity (which I would be doing if I said: divinity is born from Mary), but I am attributing both omnipotence and human birth to the one divine person who is both God and man. Especially in the Nestorian controversy, this mutual predication of properties was crucial; failure to understand it led Nestorius to attack the *theotokos* (Mary's motherhood of God) and other formulas of Christian tradition, which were really only explicitations of "The Word was made flesh."

In the final section, we will try to indicate the enduring value and importance of the fathers' contribution to our doctrinal portrait of Christ. Now, however, it is our task to enter as fully as we can into this world of long ago. It was then, amid bitter strife, that Christian reflection came to know Christ Jesus better in the very depths of his being, but to know especially that he is essentially mystery—the mystery of man joined to the mystery of God in the mystery of the God-man.

QUESTIONS FOR DISCUSSION

1. What is the basic difference between the Christology of the New Testament and the Christology of the fathers? Explain.
2. In which century did the Christological problem finally crystallize and why?
3. What is the difference in approach between the Word-flesh Christology of Alexandria and the Word-man Christology of Antioch?
4. What heresy represents the extreme form of the Word-flesh Christology? Of the Word-man Christology?
5. What soteriological axiom constantly recurs in the patristic arguments against heresies?
6. Explain what is meant by physico-mystical solidarity.
7. Explain what is meant by the mutual predication of properties. Can you give an example?

CHAPTER 1
BEFORE NICAEA

Prefatory Note

The history of Christology before Nicaea may be roughly divided into two periods: (A) that of the apostolic fathers and apologetes; and (B) that of Irenaeus and the fathers of the third century, especially the great Alexandrians, Clement and Origen, and the African, Tertullian.

The Christology of the former period is largely pastoral and untheoretical, though Justin in his apologies achieves a degree of systematization. Docetism is the primary target. There is striking use of the mutual predication of properties, especially in Ignatius and Melito. Redemption is approached especially from the viewpoint of illumination and teaching. Justin's doctrine of Christ as the Word in its fullness is here of greatest importance.

With Irenaeus we move to a more profound grasp of the mystery of Christ. His Christology is anti-docetic and anti-gnostic, and hence stresses both the reality of Christ's flesh and the fact that he is one and the same, God and man. Irenaeus' celebrated doctrine of "recapitulation," the restoration and renewal of all things through the second Adam, puts Christ at the center of history and the universe.

With the third century, trinitarian controversy comes to the fore, and Christology is largely incidental to it. Of the Alexandrians, Clement is notable for his presentation of the savior as the true gnostic and the teacher of mankind; he is led at times, however, in the direction of docetism when he removes Christ somewhat from the conditions of earthly existence. Origen puts the human soul of Christ at the center of his Christology.

In Latin Africa, Tertullian remarkably anticipates the terminology of the fifth century by speaking of Christ in terms of two substances and a single person.

With the condemnation in 268 of the adoptionism of Paul of Samosata at the synod of Antioch we have a first rumbling of the sharp Christological conflicts which would come to the fore once the Nicene trinitarian crisis had been resolved.

A. Apostolic Fathers and Apologetes

1. IGNATIUS OF ANTIOCH

Introduction

The witness to Christ of this heroic bishop of the subapostolic age comes to us in the form of seven letters, addressed to several churches of Asia Minor, to the church of Rome, and to Polycarp (also a bishop and future martyr), and written on the road to martyrdom in Rome about 110 A.D. Ignatius is above all the champion of unity. He pleads with the churches of Asia Minor for solidarity with and under their bishops. This unity of the Christian community, he says, is the reflection of the unity of God himself, of Christ with the Father, and of each Christian with Christ. More important for us here is Ignatius' teaching on the unity of Christ, which does not exclude a certain duality, but which permits Ignatius to speak of "the blood of God" (Ephesians 1), "our God Jesus Christ . . . conceived by Mary" (Ephesians 18; a striking anticipation of the famous watchword of orthodoxy, *theotokos*), and of "my suffering God" (Romans 6). Significant too is his denunciation of docetism, the view that the flesh and fleshly events of Christ's life were mere appearance. If Christ's flesh is only appearance, not reality, he argues, then our salvation is only appearance, not reality. His soteriology is close to the bible, stressing Christ's conquest of Satan and the theme of the imitation of Christ, especially in martyrdom. Finally, he suggests how the reality of Christ's flesh is essential for the Christian unity so dear to his heart: the docetists significantly remain aloof from the eucharist, the partaking of the one true flesh of Christ, which is the life and unity of the Christian community.

Ephesians 7

There is only one physician, both carnal and spiritual, born and unborn, God become man, true life in death; sprung both from Mary and from God, first subject to suffering and then incapable of it—Jesus Christ our Lord. (ACW 1.63)

Commentary: In the balanced phrases of this striking sentence, Ignatius gives early expression, in several ways, to faith in the divinity and humanity of Christ united in a single person. The *one* physician is *both* flesh *and* spirit; this is to be taken in the sense of St. Paul, for whom (cf. Rom 1:3f.) "flesh" expresses humanity, and "spirit" stands for divinity. For "God become man," another manuscript reading has "God in man." The affirmation of Mary's motherhood and of the subjection of Christ to suffering is doubtless anti-docetic.

Ephesians 18-19

The fact is, our God Jesus Christ was conceived by Mary according to God's dispensation "of the seed of David," it is true, but also of the Holy Spirit. He was born and was baptized, that by his passion he might consecrate the water. And the prince of this world was in ignorance of the virginity of Mary and her childbearing and also of the death of the Lord—three mysteries loudly proclaimed to the world, though accomplished in the stillness of God! How, then, were they revealed to the ages? A star blazed forth in the sky, outshining all the other stars, and its light was indescribable, and its novelty provoked wonderment, and all the starry orbs, with the sun and the moon, formed a choir round that star; but its light exceeded that of all the rest, and there was perplexity as to the cause of the unparalleled novelty. This was the reason why every form of magic began to be destroyed, every malignant spell to be broken, ignorance to be dethroned, an ancient empire to be overthrown—God was making his appearance in human form to mold "the newness" (Rom 6:4) of eternal life! Then at length was ushered in what God had prepared in his counsels; then all the world was in an upheaval because the destruction of death was being prosecuted. (ACW 1.67)

Commentary: This passage illustrates several aspects of patristic Christology. As in the New Testament itself (Lk 12:50), the baptism (immersion) of Christ in the waters of the Jordan and his "baptism" on Calvary are here related; the efficacy of Christian baptism derives from the power of these *mysteries.* The "silence of God" is a favorite theme of Ignatius: Christ is the Word who, in his incarnation, breaks God's silence (Magnesians 8). The theme of the *conquest* of the empire of Satan by Christ is introduced in connection with the three mysteries of Mary's virginity, her motherhood, and the death of Christ. Christ is presented as *the epiphany of God* in human form (cf. Tit 2:11; 3:4), in order *to destroy death and bring* the new *life.*

Trallians 9-11

Stop your ears therefore when anyone speaks to you that stands apart from Jesus Christ, from David's scion and Mary's son, who was really born and ate and drank, really persecuted by Pontius Pilate, really crucified and died while heaven and earth and the underworld looked on; who also really rose from the dead, since his Father raised him up—his Father, who will likewise raise us also who believe in him through Jesus Christ, apart from whom we have no real life. But if, as some atheists, that is, unbelievers, say, his suffering was but a make-believe—when, in reality, they themselves are make-believes—then why am I in chains? Why do I even pray that I may fight wild beasts? In vain, then, do I die! My testimony is, after all, but a lie about the Lord! Shun these wildlings, then, which bear but deadly fruit, and when one tastes it, he is outright doomed to die! Surely, such persons are not "the planting of the Father" [Mt 15:13]. For if they were, they would appear as branches of the cross, and their fruit would be imperishable—the cross through which by his passion he calls you to him, being members of his body. Evidently, no head can be born separately, without members, since God means complete oneness, which is himself.

(ACW 1.77-78)

Commentary: This is one of Ignatius' most vigorous attacks on docetism, which maintained that Christ did not possess true human flesh, was not truly born of Mary, did not truly suffer. Hence the frequently repeated "really," contrasted with the "make-believe" (our colloquial "phony" expresses the idea very well) doctrine of the gnostics, who feared to bring divinity into immediate contact with matter. Ignatius powerfully shows that his coming martyrdom will be without meaning unless it has roots in the true sufferings of the Lord. Note too the brief but profound expression of our oneness with Christ in his body.

Smyrnaeans 7

From eucharist and prayer they hold aloof, because they do not confess that the eucharist is the flesh of our savior Jesus Christ, which suffered for our sins, and which the Father in his loving-kindness raised from the dead. (ACW 1.92)

Commentary: Here Ignatius points out the logic of the docetists in separating themselves from the Christian assembly, in which the true flesh of Christ is eaten.

2. JUSTIN MARTYR

Introduction

Those fathers of the second century who engaged in the rational defense of Christianity against the attacks of Jews and pagans have traditionally been grouped as the apologetes. Foremost among them was St. Justin, who died a martyr about 150. His Christology, in fact his entire theology, focused on the conception of the Word, then current among stoics and others. With Clement of Alexandria and other early fathers, and in conformity with his doctrine of the Word, Justin puts special stress on the soteriological value of the teaching and example of Christ.

Second Apology 10, 13

Beyond doubt, therefore, our teachings are more noble than all human teaching, because Christ, who appeared on earth for our sakes, became the whole *Logos* [Word], namely, Logos and body and soul.

Commentary: For this important sentence we prefer the translation given by Grillmeier 109: "The Christ who has appeared for us men represents the *Logos* principle in its totality, that is both body and *Logos* and soul."

Everything that the philosophers and legislators discovered and expressed well, they accomplished through their discovery and contemplation of some part of the *Logos*. But, since they did not have a full knowledge of the *Logos,* which is Christ, they often contradicted themselves. And those who were born before Christ assumed human nature were dragged into law courts as irreligious and meddling persons, when they tried in human narrowness to think out and prove things by reason. Socrates, the most ardent of all in this regard, was accused of the very crimes that are imputed to us. They claimed that he introduced new deities and rejected the state-sponsored gods. But what he did was to ostracize Homer and the other poets, and to instruct men to expel evil demons and those who perpetrated the deeds narrated by the poets; and to exhort men by meditation to learn more about God who was unknown to them, saying: "It is not an easy matter to find the father and creator of all things, nor, when he is found, is it safe to announce him to all men" [cf. Plato, *Timaeus,* 28c]. Yet our Christ did all this through his own power. There was no one who believed so much in Socrates as to die for his teaching; but not only philosophers and scholars believed in Christ, of whom even Socrates has a vague knowledge (for he was and is the *Logos* who is in every person, and who predicted things to come through the prophets and then in person when he assumed our human nature and feelings and taught us these doctrines), but also workingmen and men wholly uneducated, who all scorned glory, and fear, and death. Indeed, this is brought about by the power of the ineffable Father, and not through the instrumentality of human reason . . . When I learned of the evil camouflage which the wicked demons had thrown around the divine doctrines of the Christians to deter others from following them, I had to laugh at the authors of these lies, at the camouflage itself, and at the popular reaction. I am proud to say that I strove with all my might to be known as a Christian, not because the teachings of Plato are different from those of Christ, but because they are not in every way similar; neither are those of other writers, the stoics, poets, and the historians. For each one of them seeing, through his participation of the seminal divine word, what was related to it, spoke very well. But they who contradict themselves in important matters evidently did not acquire the unseen [that is, heavenly] wisdom and indisputable knowledge. The truths which men in all lands have rightly spoken belong to us Christians. For we worship and love, after God the Father, the Word who is from the unbegotten and ineffable God, since he even became man for us, so that by sharing in our sufferings he might also heal us. Indeed, all writers, by means of the engrafted seed of the Word which was implanted in them, had a dim glimpse of the truth. For the seed of something and its imitation, given in proportion to one's capacity, is one thing, but the thing itself, which is shared and imitated according to his grace, is quite another. (FC 6.129-34)

Commentary: The key distinction in this capital passage is that between the partial and the complete. As God's agent in creation and revelation, the Word (*Logos*) is present in the whole world and in all men. Socrates and Plato are acknowledged to have been partial instruments of the divine Word. Only in Christ, however, is the Word present in its fullness. This conception, which affirms the uniqueness of the incarnation while relating it to the whole of humanity and to the entire cosmos, has affinities with two strong currents in today's Christology: the desire to acknowledge the value found in non-Christian religions and philosophies, and the desire for a Christocentric view of creation and a cosmic view of Christ. The sentence, "The truths which men in all lands have rightly spoken belong to us Christians," is a variation of Paul's "All things are yours" (1 Cor 3:22), and a magnificent utterance of Christian humanism.

3. MELITO OF SARDIS

Introduction

Melito, bishop of Sardis in the late second century, though a prolific writer and well known for the apology which he wrote to Emperor Marcus Aurelius in defense of Christianity, had till recently come down to us only in fragments. A few decades ago, however, the discovery of a work by him (probably a paschal homily) provided a new source for early patristic Christology. The sermon shows how the Exodus events have been fulfilled in Christ. It is rich, even ornate, in its rhetoric. The unity of Christ emerges in the powerful description of the passion. Both the body and the spirit (divinity) of the savior have their role in the destruction of suffering and death.

Homily on the Pasch 5-10, 66, 95

In place of the lamb there came God, and in place of the sheep a man; and, in the man, Christ, who contains all things. Therefore the sacrifice of the sheep and the celebration of the pasch, and the letter of the law, have issued in Christ, because of whom all was done in the old law, or rather in the new word. For the law became word, the old became new (going forth from Zion and Jerusalem), and the command became grace, and the type became reality, and the lamb became son, and the sheep became man, and man became God. For born as a son, and led forth as a lamb, and sacrificed as a sheep, and buried as a man, he rose from the dead as God, being by nature God and man. He is all things: as he who judges, he is law; as he who teaches, word; as he who saves, grace; as he who begets, father; as he who is begotten, son; as he who suffers, sheep; as he who is buried, man; as he who rises, God. This is Jesus Christ, to whom belongs the glory forever. Amen.

Commentary: Besides situating Christ in the history of salvation, these statements affirm the mystery of the incarnation. Christ is "by nature God and man." In "nature" we see the terminology which will later be officially endorsed in the two-nature teaching of Chalcedon. In Melito, however, the phrase is not to be taken philosophically; little more is meant than that Christ is *truly* God and man.

Come from heaven to earth because of suffering [man], and having put on [man] himself through the virgin Mary, and having come as a man, he took on himself the sufferings of him who suffered, through his body which was capable of suffering, and thus destroyed the sufferings of the flesh. And by his spirit, incapable of death, he slew death, slayer of men.

Commentary: Two points are worthy of note here: first, the insistence (doubtless against gnostic docetism) on the true sufferings of Christ, which by a kind of identity destroyed our sufferings; second, the recurrence of the flesh-spirit schema, which we have already encountered in Ignatius.

And so he was raised on a cross and a title was placed, indicating who it was who was being executed. Painful it is to say, but more terrible not to say. And so listen and tremble before him who made the earth tremble: he who suspended the earth is suspended; he who fixed the heavens is fixed; he who fastened all things is fastened to the wood; the master is outraged; God is murdered; the king of Israel is slain by Israel's hand. (ed. Testuz 30-35.102-5.140f.)

Commentary: This is a striking, even shocking, instance of the so-called mutual predication of properties, where a human attribute ("is murdered") is predicated of Christ, who is named according to his divinity ("God"). The usage is an implicit affirmation of unity of person in Christ, and is frequent in the Fathers.

4. THE LETTER TO DIOGNETUS

Introduction

Several aspects of redemption are illustrated in the following passage from this work, whose author and date are uncertain: the *time* of redemption, which came after centuries of man's experience of his own inability to save himself; the *principle* of redemption, the divine mercy; the element of *ransom* and "sweetest exchange." This last phrase may be compared with the *admirabile commercium* of the Latin liturgy (cf. Introit of the Mass for January 1).

Letter 8-9

After, then, he had already planned everything in his own counsels in union with the Son, he yet permitted us, all through the intervening times, to be carried away, just as we chose, by unruly passions—victims of unbridled desires! Not that he took delight in our transgressions; no, he merely exercised patience. Nor did he approve of that former era of wickedness, but, on the contrary, was all the time shaping the present era of holiness. It was his intention that we, after our conduct in the past had proved us unworthy of life, should now be rendered worthy by the goodness of God, and that, after we had demonstrated our inability, as far as in us lay, to enter the kingdom of God, should be enabled to do so by the power of God. And when the cup of our iniquities was filled, and it had become perfectly clear that their wages, the punishment of death, had to be expected, then the season arrived, during which God had determined to reveal henceforth his goodness and power. O the surpassing kindness and love of God for man! No, he did not hate us, or discard us, or remember our wrongs; he exercised forbearance and long-suffering! In mercy, of his own accord, he lifted the burden of our sins! Of his own accord he gave up his own Son as a ransom for us—the saint for sinners, the guiltless for the guilty, the innocent for the wicked, the incorruptible for the corruptible, the immortal for the mortal! Indeed, what else could have covered our sins but his holiness? In whom could we, the lawless and impious, be sanctified but in the Son of God alone? O sweetest exchange! O unfathomable accomplishment! O unexpected blessings—the sinfulness of many was buried in one who is holy, the holiness of one sanctifies the many who are sinners! (ACW 6.142-3)

B. Irenaeus and the Third-Century Fathers

1. IRENAEUS OF LYONS

Introduction

Irenaeus, bishop of Lyons (c. 180), the greatest theologian of the second century, is, like Ignatius before him, the champion of unity. His great work, *Against Heresies,* is primarily directed against various gnostic systems which maintained a series of divine marriages and emanations in such a way as to compromise both the unicity of God and the unity of Christ. Irenaeus insists strongly that God is one, and, with reference to Christ, his "one and the same" later became a central motif of the Chalcedonian definition. The unity of creation and redemption, of the old and the new dispensations, and of the entire divine plan of salvation is a prominent feature of this theology. It is in this concern for unity that his famous doctrine of "recapitulation" *(anakephalaiosis),* the consummation of all things in Christ, may best be seen. Christ the God-man came as the second Adam to restore and renew the plan of salvation which had been deprived of fulfillment by Adam's sin. Christ had to be both God and man: only God can save, and only a man by his obedience could undo the disobedience of Adam. His role was to bring God down to man and man up to God. He did this by a conquest of Satan characterized by justice and persuasion, not violence. Finally, Irenaeus is a primary witness, against gnostic docetism, to the true human flesh of Christ: only if Christ really suffered do our sufferings have meaning.

Against Heresies 3.16.6

Thus there is one God the Father, as we have demonstrated, and one Christ Jesus our Lord who came in fulfillment of God's comprehensive design and consummates all things in himself. Man is in all respects the handiwork of God; thus he consummates man in himself: he was invisible and became visible; incomprehensible and made comprehensible; impassible and made passible; the Word, and made man; consummating all things in himself. That, as in things above the heavens and in the spiritual and invisible world the Word of God is supreme, so in the visible and physical realm he may have pre-eminence, taking to himself the primacy and constituting himself the head of the Church, that he may draw all things to himself in the due time. (Bettenson[2] 110-11)

Commentary: In the invisible world it is the Word who is the head of all creation; so now, with the incarnation, the whole of the visible creation comes under the headship of the Word incarnate, especially inasmuch as he is head of the Church.

Against Heresies 3.18.6-7

If he did not really suffer there was no grace . . . and when we begin to endure real suffering he will clearly be leading us astray in exhorting us to endure scourging and to turn the other cheek, if he did not first endure the same treatment and in reality . . . in that case we should be above our master . . . But as he, our Lord, is our only true master, so he is truly the good and suffering Son of God, the Word of God the Father made the son of man. For he strove and conquered. He was as man contending on behalf of the fathers and through obedience cancelling the disobedience. He bound the strong one and set free the weak, and gave salvation to his handiwork by abolishing sin. For he is our most holy Lord, the merciful lover of the human race. He united man to God, as we have said. Had he not as man overcome man's adversary, the enemy would not have been justly overcome. Again, had it not been God who bestowed salvation, we should not have it as a secure possession. And if man had not been united to God, man could not have become a partaker of immortality. For the mediator between God and man had to bring both parties into friendship and concord through his kinship with both; and to present man to God, and make God known to man. In what way could we share in the adoption of the sons of God unless through the Son we had received the fellowship with the Father, unless the Word of God was made flesh and entered into communion with us? Therefore he passed through every stage of life, restoring to each age fellowship with God. (Bettenson[2] 107-8)

Commentary: Several points are of interest in this rich passage. First, Irenaeus echoes the anti-docetic insistence of Ignatius that our sufferings have meaning only if Christ really suffered. Secondly, we find the undoing of the disobedience of the first Adam by the obedience of the second Adam, a favorite idea of Irenaeus (echoing, of course, Rom 5:12-21). Thirdly, Irenaeus advances a theological argument for the necessity of the savior's being both God and man; this argument will be frequently taken up, most prominently, perhaps, in St. Anselm's *Why the God-Man.* Finally, there is the notion that every stage of human life has been redeemed by the fact that the Son of God embraced it.

Against Heresies 5.1.1

The powerful Word, and true man, redeeming [ransoming] us by his own blood in a reasonable way, gave himself as a ransom for those who have been led into captivity. And since the Apostasy [i.e., the rebellious spirit, Satan] unjustly held sway over us and though we were by nature [the possession] of almighty God, he estranged us against nature, making us his own disciples; therefore the Word of God, mighty in all things and not lacking in his own justice, acted justly even in the encounter with the Apostasy itself, ransoming from it that which was his own, not by force, in the way in which it secured the sway over us at the beginning, snatching insatiably what was not its own; but by persuasion, as it became God to receive what he wished; by persuasion, not by the use of force, that the principles of justice might not be infringed, and, at the same time, that God's original creation might not perish. By his own blood, then, the Lord redeemed us, and gave his life for our life, his flesh for our flesh; and he poured out the Spirit of the Father to bring about the union and communion of God and man, bringing down God to men through the Spirit while raising man to God through the incarnation, and in his advent [or, by his presence] surely and truly giving us incorruption through the communion which we have with God. (Bettenson[1] 43-44)

Commentary: Here we find, side by side, two quite different views of redemption. There is first of all the so-called *ransom* theory: in the blood of Christ shed for us God observes justice even in dealing with Satan, in that he conquers him not by violence but by persuasion; Irenaeus does not go so far as to say, as other fathers were to say, that the blood of Christ was paid to Satan as a ransom. Secondly, there is a suggestion of the *physico-mystical* notion of redemption: the incarnation represents a union and communion of man with God in which God is truly man and all men share in the incorruptibility proper to divinity. "His life for our life" is better translated "his soul for our soul": the sentence suggests the need of an integral humanity in the savior, corresponding to body and soul in man.

2. CLEMENT OF ALEXANDRIA

Introduction

Clement (d. 215), a great leader of the third-century catechetical school of Alexandria, drew on a broad cultural background and outstanding speculative powers to construct a theology of the Word. For him as previously for Justin, Christ is principally the Word in person, the teacher come to enlighten man and teach him the true gnosis. Clement's respect for the transcendence and moral perfection of Christ, together with certain influences from the stoic doctrine of human passions, leads him at times to picture the savior as unable to suffer and above the need for food.

Exhortation to the Greeks 1

Let us bring down truth, with wisdom in all her brightness, from heaven above, to the holy mountain of God and the holy company of the prophets. Let truth, sending forth her rays of light into the farthest distance, shine everywhere upon those who are wallowing in darkness, and deliver men from their error, stretching out her supreme right hand, even understanding, to point them to salvation. And when they have raised their heads and looked up let them forsake Helicon and Cithaeron to dwell in Zion; "for out of Zion shall go forth the law, and the Word of the Lord from Jerusalem" [Is 2:3], that is, the heavenly Word, the true champion, who is being crowned upon the stage of the whole world. Aye, and this Eunomus of mine sings not the strain of Terpander or of Capio, nor yet in Phrygian or Lydian or Dorian mode; but the new music, with its eternal strain that bears the name of God. This is the new song, the song of Moses, "Soother of grief and wrath, that bids all ills be forgotten" [Homer, *Odyssey* 4.221]. There is a sweet and genuine medicine of persuasion blended with this song . . .

But far different [from the pagan poets] is my minstrel, for he has come to bring to a speedy end the bitter slavery of the daemons that lord it over us; and by leading us back to the mild and kindly yoke of piety he calls once again to heaven those who have been cast down to earth . . .

See how mighty is the new song! It has made men out of stones and men out of wild beasts. They who were otherwise dead, who had no share in the real and true life, revived when they but heard the song. Furthermore, it is this which composed the entire creation into melodious order, and turned into concert the discord of the elements, that the whole universe might be in harmony with it. . . . What is more, this pure song, the stay of the universe and the harmony of all things, stretching from the center to the circumference and from the extremities to the center, reduced this whole to harmony, not in accordance with Thracian music, which resembles that of Jubal [cf. Gn 4:21], but in accordance with the fatherly purpose of God, which David earnestly sought. He who sprang from David and yet was before him, the Word of God, scorned those lifeless instruments of lyre and harp. By the power of the Holy Spirit he arranged in harmonious order this great world, yes, and the little world of man too, body and soul together; and on this many-voiced instrument of the universe he makes music to God, and sings to the human instrument . . . The Lord fashioned man a beautiful, breathing instrument, after his own image; and assuredly he himself is an all-harmonious instrument of God, melodious and holy, the wisdom that is above this world, the heavenly Word.

What then is the purpose of this instrument, the Word of God, the Lord, and the new song? To open the eyes of the blind, to unstop the ears of the deaf, and to lead the halt and erring into the way of righteousness; to reveal God to foolish men, to make an end of corruption, to vanquish death, to reconcile disobedient sons to the Father. The instrument of God is loving to men. The Lord pities, chastens, exhorts, admonishes, saves and guards us; and, over and above this, promises the kingdom of heaven as reward for our discipleship, while the only joy he has of us is that we are saved. For wickedness feeds upon the corruption of men; but truth, like the bee, does no harm to anything in the world, but takes delight only in the salvation of men. You have then God's promise; you have his love to man; partake of his grace.

And do not suppose that my song of salvation is new in the same sense as an implement or a house. For it was "before the morning star" [Ps 109:3 (LXX)]; and "in the beginning was the Word, and the Word was with God, and the Word was God" [Jn 1:1]. But error is old and truth appears to be a new thing . . . We were before the foundation of the world, we who, because we were destined to be in him, were begotten beforehand by God. We are the rational images formed by God's Word, or reason, and we date from the beginning on account of our connection with him, because "the Word was in the beginning." Well, because the Word was from the first, he was and is the divine beginning of all things; but because he lately took a name—the name consecrated of old and worthy of power, the Christ—I have called him a new song.

The Word, then, that is the Christ, is the cause both of our being long ago (for he was in God) and of our well-being. This Word, who alone is both God and man, the cause of all our good, appeared but lately in his own person to men; from whom learning how to live rightly on earth, we are brought on our way to eternal life . . . This is the new song, namely, the manifestation which has but now shined forth among us, of Him who was in the beginning, the pre-existent Word. Not long ago the pre-existent savior appeared on earth; he who exists in God [literally, "He who exists in him who exists"] (because "the Word was with God") appeared as our teacher; the Word appeared by whom all things have been created. He who gave us life in the beginning, when as creator he formed us, taught us how to live rightly by appearing as our teacher, in order that hereafter as God he might supply us with life everlasting. (LCL 7-19)

Commentary: The *Exhortation to the Greeks* is an effort to convince pagans that only in Christ will they find what they have vainly sought in mythology and philosophy. While other aspects of redemption are present, the primary stress is on the enlightenment that Christ brings to men in the new song of salvation. It is as Word and as teacher of men that Clement prefers to think of him. The cosmic dimensions of Christology are also well illustrated in this beautiful passage. The new song sung by Christ the minstrel not only brings life to dead men, but gives to the entire universe (and to the microcosm which is man) their ultimate harmony. One is reminded of Newman's lovely sermon, "The Cross of Christ the Measure of the World": the cross is "the tone into which all the strains of this world's music are ultimately to be resolved" *(Parochial and Plain Sermons* 6.85).

Miscellanies 6.9

The gnostic is such that he is subject only to the affections that exist for the maintenance of the body, such as hunger, thirst, and the like. But in the case of the savior, it would be ludicrous [to suppose] that the body demanded the necessary aids in order to extend its duration. For he ate, not for the sake of the body, which was kept together by a holy energy, but in order that it might not enter into the minds of those who were with him to entertain a different opinion of him; in like manner as certainly some afterwards supposed that he appeared in a phantasmal shape. But he was entirely impassible, inaccessible to any movement of feeling, either pleasure or pain. While the apostles, having most gnostically mastered anger and fear and lust through the Lord's teaching, were not liable even to such of the movements of feeling as seem good (courage, zeal, joy, desire) because they remained steadfast, not changing a whit, but ever continuing unvarying in a state of training after the resurrection of the Lord. And should it be granted that the affections specified above, when produced rationally, are good, yet are they inadmissible in the case of the perfect man, who is incapable of exercising courage; for neither does he meet what inspires fear, as he regards none of the things that occur in life as to be dreaded; nor can anything dislodge him from this—the love he has towards God.

(based on ANF 2.496)

Commentary: In this passage we see how stoic thought affected Clement's Christology. The ordinary gnostic or perfect Christian needs bodily *pathe* ("passions" or movements), spontaneous impulses needed to maintain bodily life; not so Christ, because the indwelling Word perceives all that is necessary for the support of the body. Clement goes so far as to deny the savior's need of bodily food. Then there are *pathe* of a more spiritual kind, movements of courage, sorrow, etc. Even the ordinary Christian, if he is to be a true gnostic, must rise above them; still more are they to be excluded from Christ, the perfect gnostic. While he does not deny the presence of a rational soul in Christ, Clement has the distinctively Alexandrian idea of the Word as the inner governing power in Christ. Later this conception will be understood by Apollinarius as excluding a rational soul. And except for Origen, none of the great Alexandrians (Clement, Athanasius, or Cyril) give the human soul of Christ an adequate place in their soteriology, or savior-theology. Antiochene and Latin Christology will supply for this lack.

The Educator 1.9.83-4

Just as those who are well do not need a physician in that they are strong, but only those who are sick [cf. Lk 5:31] and in need of his skill, so, too, we need the savior because we are sick from the reprehensible lusts of our lives, and from blameworthy vices and from the diseases caused by our other passions. He applies not only remedies that soothe, but also others that sear, such as the bitter herb of fear which arrests the growth of sin. Fear, then, is bitter, but it confers health. Truly, then, we need the savior, for we are sick; the guide, for we are wandering; him who gives light, for we are blind; the life-giving spring, for we are parched with thirst, and, once we have tasted of it, we will never thirst again. We are in need of life, for we are dead; of the shepherd, for we are sheep; of the educator, for we are children. In a word, throughout the whole of our human lives, we need Jesus that we may not go astray and at length merit condemnation as sinners . . .

Feed us, your little ones, for we are your sheep! Yes, O master, fill us with your food, your justice. Yes, O educator, shepherd us to your holy mountain, the church, which is lifted up above the clouds, touching the heavens. (FC 23.74-5)

Commentary: Different aspects of redemption are here summarily suggested. The title of the work expresses, however, what is for Clement primary: Christ is the unique teacher.

3. ORIGEN

Introduction

The theology of Origen (d. 255), gives primacy to created souls (which he thinks of as eternally pre-existent) and their freedom to choose good and evil. His Christology also centers on the human soul of Christ as mediating agent in our salvation. The one soul which was destined to be the soul of the Word incarnate was like other souls in all things except the perfection of its burning love of the Word, which made it completely sinless. It was only by union with this soul at a moment of time that the Word could be united with flesh. Despite his insistence on the sinlessness of Christ, Origen attributes to him in his earthly state ignorance, suffering, and temptation. Origen, who has a strongly mystical tendency, holds that the man Jesus is progressively divinized. Thus, in a functional or, better, moral and spiritual sense, Jesus ceases, with the resurrection, to be man. Now he is God. This transformation of Christ is the pattern for the divinization of the Christian.

Despite its many awkward expressions, the Christology of Origen is basically orthodox, and his brilliant pen has given us some of the classic Christological terms. He was, with Clement, the first to use the trinitarian *homoousios* (the persons are "consubstantial" with one another), and he coined the term "God-man" *(theanthropos)*. Further, he domesticated the term *nature* and other terms used in the theology of Christ. His soteriology is couched principally in the language of illumination and mystical transformation. But he also conceives of redemption as a conquest of and ransom paid to Satan, and as a sacrifice.

First Principles 2.6

Of all the marvellous and mighty acts related of him, this altogether surpasses human admiration, and is beyond the power of mortal frailness to understand or feel, how that mighty power of divine majesty, that very Word of the Father, and that very wisdom of God, in which were created all things, visible and invisible, can be believed to have existed within the limits of that man who appeared in Judea; nay, that the wisdom of God can have entered the womb of a woman, and have been born an infant, and have uttered wailings like the cries of little children! And that afterwards it should be related that he was greatly troubled in death, saying, as he himself declared, "My soul is sorrowful, even unto death" [Mt 26:38]; and that at the last he was brought to that death which is accounted the most shameful among men, although he rose again on the third day. Since, then, we see in him some things so human that they appear to differ in no respect from the common frailty of mortals, and some things so divine that they can appropriately belong to nothing else than to the primal and ineffable nature of deity, the narrowness of human understanding can find no outlet; but, overcome with the amazement of a mighty admiration, knows not whither to withdraw, or what to take hold of, or whither to turn. If it thinks of a God, it sees a mortal; if it thinks of a man, it beholds him returning from the grave, after overthrowing the empire of death, laden with its spoils. And therefore the spectacle is to be contemplated with all fear and reverence, that the truth of both natures may be clearly shown to exist in one and the same being; so that nothing unworthy or unbecoming may be perceived in that divine and ineffable substance, nor yet those things which were done be supposed to be the illusions of imaginary appearances. . . .

Commentary: The last sentence formulates the mystery of Christ as two natures in one and the same being, and shows Origen's sensitivity to the need of keeping both perfect divinity and true humanity uncompromised in our conception of Christ.

The only-begotten of God, therefore, through whom, as the previous course of the discussion has shown, all things were made, visible and invisible, according to the view of scripture, both made all things and loves what he made. For since he is himself the invisible image of the invisible God, he conveyed invisibly a share in himself to all his rational creatures, so that each one obtained a part of him exactly proportioned to the amount of affection with which he [the rational creature] regarded him [the only-begotten of God]. But since, agreeably to the faculty of free will, variety and diversity characterized the individual souls, so that one was attached with a warmer love to the author of its being, and another with a feebler and weaker regard, that soul regarding which Jesus said, "No one shall take my life from me" [Jn 10:18], inhering, from the beginning of the creation, and afterwards, inseparably and indissolubly in him, as being the wisdom and Word of God, and the truth and the true light, and receiving him wholly, and passing into his light and splendor, was made with him in a preeminent degree one spirit, according to the promise of the apostle to those who ought to imitate it that "he who is joined in the Lord is one spirit" [1 Cor 6:17]. This substance of a soul, then, being intermediate between God and the flesh —it being impossible for the nature of God to intermingle with a body without an intermediate instrument—the God-man is born, as we have said, that substance being the intermediary to whose nature it was not contrary to assume a body. But neither, on the other hand, was it opposed to the nature of that soul, as a rational existence, to receive God, into whom, as stated above, as into the Word, and the wisdom, and the truth, it had already wholly entered. And therefore deservedly is it also called, along with the flesh which it had assumed, the Son of God, and the power of God, the Christ, and the wisdom of God, either because it was wholly in the Son of God, or because it received the Son of God wholly into itself.

Commentary: This passage expresses Origen's distinctive notion of the human soul of Christ, united eternally with the Word in a union of perfect love which renders it sinless, and, at the moment of the incarnation, mediating the Word's union with flesh. As created soul it is itself capable of union with flesh; and, as a rational existence, it is likewise capable of receiving the Word in intimate union.

And again, the Son of God, through whom all things were created, is named Jesus Christ and the son of man. For the Son of God is said to have died—in reference, namely, to that nature which could admit of death; and he is called the son of man, who is announced as about to come in the glory of God the Father with the holy angels. And for this reason, throughout the whole of scripture, not only is the divine nature spoken of in human words, but the human nature is adorned by appellations of divine dignity. More truly indeed of this than of any other can the statement be affirmed, "They shall both be in one flesh, and are no longer two, but one flesh" [Gn 2:24; cf. Mk 10:8]. For the Word of God is to be considered as being more in one flesh with the soul than a man with his wife. But to whom is it more becoming to be also one spirit with God, than to this soul which has so joined itself to God by love that it may justly be said to be one spirit with him?

Commentary: Here Origen both affirms the principle of the mutual predication of properties, and applies to the incarnation the biblical analogy of bridal union.

Now, if our having shown above that Christ possessed a rational soul should cause a difficulty to anyone, seeing we have frequently proved throughout all our discussions that the nature of souls is capable both of good and evil, the difficulty will be explained in the following way. That the nature, indeed, of his soul was the same as that of all others cannot be doubted; otherwise it could not be called a soul were it not truly one. But since the power of choosing good and evil is within the reach of all, this soul which belonged to Christ elected to love righteousness, so that in proportion to the immensity of its love it clung to it unchangeably and inseparably, so that firmness of purpose, and immensity of affection, and an inextinguishable warmth of love destroyed all susceptibility for alteration and change; and that which formerly depended upon the will was changed by the power of long custom into nature; and so we must believe that there existed in Christ a human and rational soul, without supposing that it had any feeling or possibility of sin.

In this way, then, that soul which, like an iron in the fire, has been perpetually placed in the Word, and perpetually in the wisdom, and perpetually in God, is God in all that it does, feels and understands, and therefore can be called neither convertible nor mutable, inasmuch as, being incessantly heated, it possessed immutability from its union with the Word of God. To all the saints, finally, some warmth from the Word of God must be supposed to have passed; and in this soul the divine fire itself must be believed to have rested, from which some warmth may have passed to others. (ANF 4.281-3)

Commentary: Here Origen meets the problem still faced today: how the human freedom of Christ is compatible with his absolute sinlessness. The solution he finds in the fact that the unique intensity of this unique soul's love for the Word brings an adhesion which is equivalently the very nature of the soul, so that sin becomes an impossibility.

Homilies on Luke 29

Therefore if the Son of God, himself God, was made man for you and is tempted, you, a man by nature, have no right to be aggrieved if you happen to be tempted. And if in temptation you imitate him who was tempted for you and overcome every temptation, your hope then lies with him who was once a man but has now ceased to be a man . . . For if he who once was man, after he had been tempted and the devil departed from him till the time of his death, on arising from the dead shall die no more, whereas every man is subject to death, he consequently who dies no more is no longer man but God. And if he who once was man is God, you too must be like him, for we shall be like him and we shall see him as he is. You too must become a god in Christ Jesus, to whom be the glory and the dominion forever and ever. (Tollinton 120)

Commentary: This and the following passage bring out that Origen is more interested in the action of Christ and in the mystical union of his soul with the Word than in his metaphysical constitution. With his glorification Christ ceases to be man and is now God; and we must follow him on this road of mystic transformation.

Commentary on John 32.25

The glory because of death at the hands of man is not the glory of him who by nature could not die, the only-begotten Word and wisdom and truth . . . but the glory of the man, who was also son of man, born of the seed of David according to the flesh [Rom 1:3] . . . It is he, I think, made obedient unto death, even the death of the cross, whom God exalted [cf. Phil 2:8f.]. For the Word who in the beginning was with God [cf. Jn 1:1], God the Word, could not be further exalted. The exaltation of the son of man, which came to him for his glorifying God by his death, was this, that he was no longer distinct from the Word but absolutely one with him. For if "he who is joined to the Lord is one spirit" [1 Cor 6:17] so that of him and of the Holy Spirit it can no longer be said that they are two, how much more may we not say that the humanity of Jesus became one with the Word? For he was exalted who did not consider his being equal to God robbery, and the Word remained in, or was restored to, his own glory when he was again with God, this Word of God who was man.
(ed. GCS 4.470)

Commentary: Here too the exaltation of Christ is conceived as bringing perfect mystical union between the son of man and the Word. Origen's distinction between the Word and the man is a manner of speaking which was discountenanced in the condemnation of Nestorius.

Dialogue with Heraclides

Our savior and Lord, wishing to save man in the way in which he wished to save him, for this reason desired in this way to save the body, just as it was likewise his will to save also the soul; he also wished to save the remaining part of man, the spirit. The whole man would not have been saved unless he had taken upon him the whole man. They do away with the salvation of the human body when they say that the body of the savior is spiritual. They do away with the salvation of the human spirit, concerning which the apostle says: "No man knows the things of man except the spirit of man that is in him" [1 Cor 2:11] . . . Because it was his will to save the spirit of man, about which the apostle said this, he also assumed the spirit of man. (LCC 2.442)

Commentary: Origen here repeats the soteriological argument for the assumption of a complete humanity by the Word. He follows a theory which views man as divided into three parts—body, soul and spirit.

4. TERTULLIAN

Introduction

Though Tertullian died in 220, two centuries before Ephesus and Chalcedon, his Christological vocabulary anticipated in remarkable detail the terminology that Chalcedon definitively endorsed. He speaks of one person and of two substances, states, and qualities in Christ. His *Salva est utriusque proprietas substantiae* ("The proper being of each substance remains unimpaired") will be echoed in the Chalcedonian era by Pope Leo's *salva igitur proprietate utriusque naturae* ("with the proper being of each nature left unimpaired"). The later formula, however, will be the expression of a deeper speculative penetration than Tertullian achieved.

Like most of the fathers, Tertullian showed a deep concern in his Christology for the humanity of the savior, and its role in our salvation. His work, *The Flesh of Christ,* is a refutation of the docetism of the gnostics.

The Flesh of Christ 5

There are, I submit, other things, too, that are foolish enough, those concerned with the reproaches and sufferings of God. If not, let them call it prudence that God was crucified. Excise this also, Marcion—or rather, this for preference. For which is more beneath God's dignity, more a matter of shame, to be born or to die, to carry about a body or a cross, to be circumcised or to be crucified, to be fed at the breast or to be buried, to be laid in a manger or to be entombed in a sepulcher? You will be wiser if you also refuse to believe these. Yet wise you cannot be, except by becoming a fool in the world through believing the foolish things of God . . . Spare the one and only hope of the whole world: why tear down the indispensable dishonor of the faith? Whatever is beneath God's dignity is for my advantage. I am saved if I am not ashamed of my Lord . . . The Son of God was crucified: I am not ashamed —because it is shameful. The Son of God died: it is immediately credible—because it is silly. He was buried, and rose again: it is certain—because it is impossible.

Commentary: Though Tertullian never uttered the famous phrase often attributed to him: *Credo quia absurdum* ("I believe because it is nonsense"), he here says the equivalent. By temperament fond of paradox, he did not share the speculative thirst of the Alexandrians; nor did he feel compelled to bring faith and philosophy into harmony.

But how can these acts be true in him, if he himself was not true, if he had not truly in himself that which could be crucified, which could die, which could be buried and raised up again—this flesh, in fact, suffused with blood, scaffolded of bones, threaded through with sinews, intertwined with veins, competent to be born and to die, human unquestionably, as born of a human mother? . . .

Commentary: Here Tertullian vigorously combats docetism, and insists on the truth of the sufferings of Christ. Elsewhere this same concern for the true humanity of Christ led him to deny the virginity of Mary in and after the birth of the savior.

Thus the official record of both substances represents him as both man and God: on the one hand born, on the other hand not born; on the one hand fleshly, on the other spiritual; on the one hand weak, on the other exceeding strong: on the one hand dying, on the other living. That these two sets of attributes, the divine and the human, are each kept distinct from the other, is of course accounted for by the equal verity of each nature, both flesh and spirit being in full degree what they claim to be: the powers of the spirit of God proved him God, the sufferings proved there was the flesh of man. If the powers postulate the spirit, no less do the sufferings postulate the flesh. If the flesh along with the sufferings was fictitious, it follows that the spirit also along with the powers was a fraud. Why make out that Christ was half a lie? He was wholly the truth. (Evans[1] 17-21)

Commentary: In pursuing his argument against docetism, Tertullian insists on the doctrine of the two natures of Christ, who is both man and God. Note that he makes use of the flesh-spirit antithesis; as in Ignatius, "spirit" stands for the divine.

Against Praxeas 27

We must also enquire about this, how the Word was made flesh, whether as transformed into flesh or as having clothed himself with flesh. Certainly as having clothed himself . . . For if the Word was made flesh as the result of a transformation or mutation of substance, Jesus will then be one substance [composed] of two, flesh and spirit, a kind of mixture, as electrum is [composed] of gold and silver: and he begins to be neither gold (that is, spirit) nor silver (that is, flesh), seeing that the one thing is changed by the other and a third thing is brought into being. In that case Jesus will not be God, for he has ceased to be the Word, since it has become flesh: neither will his manhood be flesh, for it is not properly flesh, seeing it has been the Word. Thus out of both things there is neither: there is some third thing far other than both.

Commentary: Tertullian here poses two alternative understandings of the incarnation, and rejects the one which would involve a transformation of the Word into flesh as a denial of two substances in Jesus, since from a transformation there would result some third reality, as in the mixture of gold and silver. Here again we see that his is a two-nature Christology; this is a general characteristic of the West, as also of Antioch.

Yet we find that he is . . . set forth as both God and man . . . without doubt according to each substance as it is distinct in what itself is, because neither is the Word anything else but God nor the flesh anything else but man. Thus also the apostle teaches of both his substances: "Who was made," he says, "of the seed of David"—here he will be man, and Son of Man; "Who was defined as Son of God according to the Spirit" [Rom 1: 3-4]—here he will be God, and the Word, the Son of God. We observe a double quality, not confused but combined, Jesus in one person God and man. I postpone the consideration of "Christ." And to such a degree did there remain unimpaired the proper being of each substance, that in him the spirit carried out its own acts, that is, powers and works and signs, while the flesh accomplished its own passions, hungering in company of the devil [Mt 4:2], thirsting in company of the Samaritan woman [Jn 4:7], weeping for Lazarus [Jn 11:35], sore troubled unto death [Mt 26:38]—and at length it also died. But if there had been some third thing, a confusion of both, like electrum, there would not be in evidence such distinct proofs of both substances; but the spirit would have performed the functions of the flesh and the flesh the functions of the spirit, by interchange, or else neither those of the flesh nor those of the spirit but those of some third form, by confusion; yes, either the Word would have died or the flesh would not have died, if the Word had been converted into flesh, for either the flesh would have been immortal or the Word mortal. But because both substances acted distinctively, each in its own quality, therefore to them accrued both their own activities and their own destinies . . . Flesh does not become spirit nor spirit flesh: evidently they can both be in one person. Of these Jesus is composed, of flesh as man and of spirit as God. (Evans [2] 173-74)

Commentary: This is doubtless the most quoted paragraph of Tertullian's Christology, for in it he speaks at the same time: 1. of a double condition or quality or state in Christ, along with the persevering presence in him of the characteristics and proper operations of each substance; 2. of Jesus as God and man *in one person*. It will take the East a few centuries more to come to the equivalent formulation of one person in two natures. One may also profitably compare certain statements of the *Tome* of Leo the Great with Tertullian's formulation. It should be pointed out, however, that Tertullian was not explicitly meeting the problem of the unity in diversity of the God-man; his problem was rather a trinitarian one, and he was concerned with refuting the position which saw in Christ a composite being made up of God the Father and the man Jesus, in one person. Tertullian's chief point is that Christ is a person distinct from the Father.

5. PAUL OF SAMOSATA AND THE SYNOD OF ANTIOCH

Introduction

In 268, a synod at Antioch condemned the doctrine of Paul of Samosata. The available sources do not permit a firm judgment as to precise issues and positions. But it seems likely that Paul professed a kind of modalistic adoptionism, according to which the Word, who is not a person distinct from the Father (modalism), indwelt in the man Jesus who, because of this indwelling, was Son (adoptionism). Mary gave birth to the Son, not to the Word. In this position we see already the divisive tendency of Antiochene Christology, which will eventually be met by the condemnation of Nestorius at Ephesus. According to some scholars, Paul's opponents may have slipped into the opposite extreme of denying a human mind in Christ, thus paving the way for Apollinarius, who did in fact refer back to this synod of 268 for support.

Synod of Antioch

Fragment 7. [Paul] Jesus Christ and the Word are other and other.

Commentary: Compare this "other and other" formulation with the resounding "one and the same" which we have noted in Irenaeus and which Chalcedon will employ. Here we have in brief and untechnical formulations the basic Christological issue: Are the eternal Word, the eternal Son of God, and Mary's son one and the same "he" or is each a distinct "he"?

Fragment 26. [Paul] A man is anointed, the Word is not anointed. The Nazarene is anointed our Lord. For the Word was greater than the Christ. For Christ became great through wisdom. The Word indeed is from above; Jesus Christ, man, is from below. Mary did not beget the Word, for Mary did not exist before the ages. Mary is not older than the Word, but gave birth to a man equal to us, but better in every respect because from the Holy Spirit.

Commentary: Here again the basic issue is seen. For Paul the man and the Word are not one and the same "he"; it follows that Mary is not mother of the Word but only of the man distinct from the Word.

Fragment 30. [The synod] What does it mean to say that the constitution of Jesus Christ is different from ours? We recognize only one difference, admittedly a very important one, between his constitution and ours, namely that the divine Word is in him what the interior man is in us.

(ed. H. de Riedmatten 137.153.154-5)

Commentary: Here the synod seems to employ the soul-body union as comparable to the union in Christ of divinity and humanity. The comparison has a long and varied history, and is employed in the *Quicumque,* one of our most important credal statements (See Chapter 3 below). It is not clear that the synod wishes to imply that the divine Word takes the place of the human mind in Christ, as Apollinarius was later to hold. The soul-body comparison is used by theologians of both Antiochene and Alexandrian tendencies.

QUESTIONS FOR DISCUSSION

1. What predominant themes characterize the writings of Ignatius of Antioch?
2. Against which heresy were Ignatius' attacks directed? Illustrate.
3. Who were the apologetes? Who figured most prominently among them?
4. In the selection from Justin's *Second Apology,* there are two trends of thought which have strong affinities to currents in today's Christology. Explain the relationships.
5. When Melito of Sardis writes that "God is murdered," what does he implicitly affirm?

6. Toward what type of heresy was Irenaeus' *Against Heresies* chiefly directed?
7. Explain Irenaeus' argument for the necessity of the savior's being both God and man.
8. In Irenaeus we find two different conceptions of redemption. Illustrate the two from Irenaeus' writings and explain the difference.
9. How did stoic thought affect Clement of Alexandria's Christology?
10. In developing his Christology, what characteristic of Christ does Clement emphasize?
11. What were some of the contributions of Origen to the historical development of Christology?
12. How does Origen reconcile Christ's human freedom and his absolute sinlessness?
13. What is Tertullian's main point in the famous passage from his work *Against Praxeas* in which he explains the unity of Christ's divinity and humanity?
14. What is the significance of the "other and other" Christological formulation of Paul of Samosata? With what formulation is it compared?

CHAPTER 2
FROM NICAEA TO CHALCEDON

Prefatory Note

For convenience we have divided the period from 325 to 451, the golden age of the fathers and of trinitarian and Christological development, into three sections. In the first, the focus is on the Word-flesh Christology of Alexandria, and the difficulty it experienced in giving full weight to the human mind of Christ. In orthodox form the Word-flesh conception occurs in Athanasius, in heterodox form in Apollinarius. The two Cappadocian Gregorys illustrate the refutation of Apollinarianism through the soteriological axiom, "What is not assumed is not healed." And in them, as well as in Athanasius, we see exemplified the physico-mystical conception of redemption. Cyril of Jerusalem is valuable for showing the liturgical and catechetical approach to Christ.

In the second section of this chapter we turn to examine the Christology of the West. Although the East remained the central arena for the great trinitarian and Christological debates, the West made occasional contributions. Its doctrine of Christ is of further interest because of its impact, especially through Augustine, on our own thinking. Tertullian's "nature" and "person" had little impact until Augustine's time. Pope Damasus interests us for his participation in the rejection of Apollinarianism; Hilary of Poitiers for the tendency (not wholly dissimilar to that already noted in Clement of Alexandria) towards docetism, but also for expressing in the West (which in general is more juridically and morally inclined than the East) the physico-mystical conception of redemption. While Ambrose and Jerome are of merely passing interest, Augustine is cited at greater length than his role in the Christological crisis of the fifth century would seem to warrant. We have given him prominence because of his influence on the Middle Ages, and also because he integrates his Christology with his doctrine of grace and other central themes.

The third section brings us to the heart of the great Christological debate. The three great Antiochenes—Diodore, Theodore and Nestorius—serve to illustrate the Word-man Christology of that school. The key figure of Cyril of Alexandria then appears on the scene with a version of the Word-flesh Christology which triumphs at Ephesus. When Cyril's extreme followers refuse to go along with the compromise between Cyril and John of Antioch, the *Formula of Union,* the monophysite crisis is on, and, with timely help from Pope Leo's *Tome to Flavian,* the stage is set for the most important single document in our volume, the definition of Chalcedon.

A. The East through the Apollinarian Controversy

1. ATHANASIUS

Introduction

The great champion of the Church against the Arians, Athanasius (d. 373), is in his soteriology deeply concerned with the divinity of the Son. If the Son is, as the Arians maintain, a creature, then he cannot save us, for only God can save. He is one of the foremost exponents of the physico-mystical conception of redemption. Because the Word is physically united with Christ's human flesh, which is in mystical solidarity with all men, that flesh and its deeds are salvific. On the constitution of Christ, Athanasius follows the Word-flesh schema characteristic of Alexandria. While no certain evidence can be adduced to show that he denied a human soul in Christ (as did his friend Apollinarius), he gives Christ's soul no significant place in his theology. This was a deficiency which the Christology of Antioch and of the West remedied; it was offset by Athanasius' clear safeguarding of the unity of Christ.

The Incarnation of the Word 9

For the Word perceived that not otherwise could the corruption of men be undone save by death as a necessary condition, while it was impossible for the Word to suffer death, being immortal and Son of the Father; to this end he takes to himself a body capable of death, that it, by partaking of the Word who is above all, might be worthy to die in the place of all, and might, because of the Word which was come to dwell in it, remain incorruptible, and that thenceforth corruption might be stayed from all by the grace of the resurrection. Whence, by offering unto death the body he himself had taken, as an offering and sacrifice free from any stain, straightway he put away death from all his peers by the offering of an equivalent. For being over all, the Word of God naturally, by offering his own temple and corporeal instrument for the life of all, satisfied the debt by his death. And thus he, the incorruptible Son of God, being conjoined with all by a like nature, naturally clothed all with incorruption, by the promise of the resurrection. For the actual corruption in death no longer has holding ground against men, by reason of the Word, which by his one body has come to dwell among them. (LCC 3.63)

Commentary: Athanasius pays a great deal of attention to the conquest of death and corruption by the death of the incorruptible Word. The solidarity of all men with Christ implicit in this conquest is conceived both in physico-mystical and in juridical terms.

The Incarnation of the Word 15-16

As a kind teacher who cares for his disciples, if some of them cannot profit by higher subjects, comes down to their level, and teaches them at any rate by simpler courses, so also did the Word of God . . . For seeing that men, having rejected the contemplation of God, and with their eyes downward, as though sunk in the deep, were seeking about for God in nature and in the world of sense, feigning gods for themselves of mortal men and demons; to this end the loving and general savior of all, the Word of God, takes to himself a body, and as a man walks among men and meets the senses of all men halfway, to the end, I say, that they who think that God is corporeal may from what the Lord effects by his body perceive the truth, and through him recognize the Father. So men as they were, and humans in all their thoughts, on whatever objects they fixed their senses, there they saw themselves met halfway, and taught the truth from every side . . . For men's minds having finally fallen to things of sense, the Word disguised himself by appearing in a body, that he might, as man, transfer men to himself, and center their senses on himself, and, men seeing him thenceforth as man, persuade them by the works he did that he is not man only, but also God, and the Word and wisdom of the true God . . . For by the Word revealing himself everywhere, both above and beneath, and in the depth and in the breadth—above, in the creation; beneath, in becoming man; in the depth, in Hades; and in the breadth, in the world—all things have been filled with the knowledge of God. Now for this cause also, he did not immediately upon his coming accomplish his sacrifice on behalf of all, by offering his body to death and raising it again, for by this means he would have made himself invisible. But he made himself visible enough by what he did, abiding in it, and doing such works, and showing such signs, as made him known no longer as man, but as God the Word. For by his becoming man, the savior was to accomplish both works of love: first in putting away death from us and renewing us again; secondly, being unseen and invisible, in manifesting and making himself known by his works to be the Word of the Father, and the ruler and king of the universe. (LCC 3.69-70)

Commentary: Here we have an example of the idea, frequent in the fathers, of salvation through divine pedagogy, which makes use of visible things to save mankind enslaved to the visible by sin. It is the flesh of Christ, rather than his human soul, which thus mediates the saving power of the Word, and it does so as a kind of sacrament manifesting the Word.

Second Oration against the Arians 69-70

Had the Son been a creature, he could not have effected our union with God, and consequently man would have had to remain mortal. A creature does not possess the power to join itself or other creatures to God; and no created being can save itself, much less can it be the author of another creature's salvation. And therefore to provide for this also God sent his Son, who, taking our nature upon him, became the son of man, that he, who was not one of us sinners, might lay down his life as a ransom for us all who were guilty and under the sentence of death; that so the justice of God might be satisfied by our undergoing the sentence in him (for all died in Christ), and thus we might all be freed from sin, and from the curse which it brought with it; and that even our bodies, being released from death, might put on immortality and incorruption, and, in union with our souls, live forever in perfect bliss . . . But all this would not have happened, if the Word had been a creature. For the devil, being himself a creature, would have ever maintained a struggle with one that was a creature like himself; and man meanwhile would have to have stood, as it were, between the two, unable to help himself, as a captive given over to death; and as being utterly destitute of any virtue capable of exalting his nature into union with God, without which he could not possibly attain to a state of happiness and security. So that the truth shows us clearly that the Word of God cannot be a creature, and that he cannot but be our Creator. For, as he had at first created and formed this body of ours, so now he assumed it to make it, as it were, over again, to communicate a divine nature to it by making it a part of himself, and did this that he might introduce us all into the kingdom of heaven after his likeness. Our nature could not have been thus joined to the divine by virtue of any conjunction with a creature, unless the Son were truly God; nor could man have been introduced into the Father's presence, unless he had been his natural and true Word, who had assumed our nature. As, on the one hand, we could not have been redeemed from sin and the curse, unless the flesh and nature, which the Word took upon him, had been truly ours (for we would have had no interest by his assumption of any foreign nature); so also man could not have been united to the divine nature, unless that Word, which was made flesh, had been, in essence and nature, the Word and Son of God. For that was the very purpose and end of our Lord's incarnation, that he should join what is by nature man to him who is by nature God, so that man might enjoy his salvation and his union with God without any fear of its failing or decrease. And, therefore, those that deny that the Son of God is properly so, of his Father's nature and substance, have as much reason to deny that he was conceived truly and properly man, of the substance of Mary ever virgin. For he would have been quite as unqualified for that work of grace, which was the occasion of his coming among us, if he had not been of the very nature of his Father, as if he had not assumed a true and proper body. And, therefore, all the raving of Valentinus will never make us believe that the Word of God is not really and truly a man; as the Arians, on the other hand, madden themselves to no purpose to make it believed that he is not properly and truly God. Having made himself man for us, he became the beginning of a new creation, a new way to bring us to happiness by what he did and suffered for us in the flesh. (based on LFC 19.163-5)

Commentary: We have here a lengthy example of how the soteriological principle was employed by Athanasius against the Arians to establish the true divinity of Christ. Note especially his great skill in likening the Arians to Valentinus, an early gnostic who denied the reality of the flesh of Christ. Just as we are not saved if Christ is not truly man with a true human body, so we are not saved if he is not truly God. What is missing in Athanasius' conception of redemptive incarnation is a significant place for the human soul of Christ. It will be the Cappadocians, especially Gregory of Nazianzus, who will fill this lacuna, through their polemic against the denial of a human soul in Christ by the Arians and Apollinarians.

Tome of the Synod of Alexandria (A.D. 362) to the Antiochenes 7

Since there has been some dispute about the incarnation of the savior, we questioned both sides. The one side accepted what the other proposed: that the Word of the Lord did not come into a holy man at the end of time in the same way that he had come to the prophets, but that the very Word was made flesh, and, though he was in the form of God, he took the form of a slave and was made man for us from Mary according to the flesh; and so the human race has been completely and perfectly freed from sin in him and quickened from death unto the kingdom of heaven. And they likewise confessed that the savior did not have a body without a soul [without life?] or feeling or intelligence. For it was not possible, when the Lord had become man for us, that his body should be without intelligence; for not only to our body but to our soul salvation came in the Word himself. And though he was truly Son of God he came to be son of man; and though he was the only-begotten Son of God he became the first-born of many brethren. And so the Son of God was not one being before Abraham and another after Abraham, nor one being while he raised Lazarus and another who asked about him. It was he who said as man: "Where has Lazarus been laid?" and who as God raised him up. It was the same one who used his body as man to spit but his divinity as Son of God to open the eyes of the man born blind. In his flesh he suffered, as Peter said [1 Pet 4:1] but in his Godhead he opened the tombs and raised the dead. (PG 26.804-805)

Commentary: This document came from a synod at Alexandria in 362 at which Athanasius sought to reconcile several trinitarian factions of Antioch. Most of the paragraph cited is anti-adoptionist: it insists that the Word did not merely dwell in Christ as in the prophets, but became man, so that one and the same Word acted humanly and divinely. The two sentences beginning "And they likewise . . ." have been adduced as a clear affirmation by Athanasius of the presence in Christ of a human mind. But it has been suggested that the sentences are a later interpolation. In addition, it is not certain in the text that the mind which the savior needed to have if he was to save our soul was the created mind as found in other men, and not the Word himself fulfilling in Christ the role which the human mind fulfills in other men. The Apollinarians accepted this paragraph as conforming to their views, and it is not an unambiguous witness to Athanasius' acceptance of a human soul in Christ.

2. APOLLINARIUS

Introduction

Apollinarius, bishop of Laodicaea (d. ca. 390), vigorously combated the Arian denial of the divinity of the Son. But he was one with the Arians in denying a human mind in Christ. This position was part of a doctrine which represented a reaction against the adoptionist currents stemming from Paul of Samosata. A human *logos* (reason) in Christ in addition to the divine *Logos* would mean that the Word was in a man, not that the Word was made flesh. For Apollinarius the divine Word is the unique life-giving principle of the flesh of Christ. Hence Christ is the heavenly man, not in the sense that his flesh came from heaven (a false accusation made against Apollinarius), but in the sense that it is the divine Word, not a human mind, which, joined to the flesh, first constitutes Christ as a man. It follows that there is only one nature in Christ, as the flesh by itself is not a nature. Arianism was more logical, it would seem, in conceiving that this immediate vitalizing of the flesh by the Word implied that the Word was not truly God. The Apollinarian position safeguards the unity of Christ against Paul of Samosata and later Antiochene positions, but only at the expense of the Word's transcendence and the integrity of Christ's human nature. Apollinarius was opposed most effectively by the Cappadocian Gregorys, and was condemned by Pope Damasus and by the First Council of Constantinople in 381.

On the Union of the Body with the Divinity in Christ

He was not conceived in the womb apart from the divinity but united with it . . . And he came down from heaven, and was not merely born of woman . . . It is not correct to call his body a creature since it is utterly inseparable from him whose body it is, and shares in the name of the uncreated one, and in being called God, because it is joined in unity to God. We must, of course, not only attribute to the body glorious things because of its divine assumption and unity with God, but also not deny the lowly traits which belong to the body, since they truly exist, because he is universally called man and the son of man, and the generations from Abraham after which he became man are enumerated. We must speak about him and hear him spoken about in human fashion. Hence when the whole of him is called man no one should deny that the divine substance is there. It is connoted along with the body by that word "man." And when he is called a servant according to the body no one should deny his nature as Lord which is meant along with the body when the word "servant" is spoken. And again when he is called the heavenly man no one should deny that the earthly body is there united with the divinity. There is no division either in fact or in name when the Lord is called a servant and when the uncreated one is called created, because of his being joined with the form of a servant [cf. Phil 2:7] and with a created body. Concerning Christ we hold that he is a created being in union with an uncreated being, an uncreated being in mixture with a created being; that he has a single nature compounded of those two parts, the Word supplying as its part the power for the forming of a whole with divine perfection. The same process takes place in any man. He is composed of two incomplete parts which make one complete nature which is designated by one name; the whole is called flesh without denying that there is a soul in it, and the whole is likewise called a soul without denying the body even though he is something more than a soul. (ed. H. Lietzmann 185-7)

Commentary: Here Apollinarius, like many of the fathers, uses the union in man of soul and body to further our understanding of the incarnation. In orthodox Christology, however, the unity in Christ is one of person only, not of nature.

Demonstration of the Incarnation of God in the Image of Man

How can God become man without ceasing to be God except by taking the place of the mind in man? (ed. Lietzmann 229)

Recapitulation

Every man is part of the world and no part of the world takes away the sin of the world since it is itself subject to sin. But

Christ takes away [the sin of the world]. Therefore Christ is not man . . . Every man is subject to death and no one subject to death abolishes death. But Christ abolishes death. Therefore Christ is not man.

Commentary: Here we have two examples of Apollinarius' use of the soteriological argument. He is not really denying that Christ is a man, but only that he is constituted man in the way we are, by a union of a human soul and flesh.

In every man mind and flesh are at odds. But in Christ they are not. Therefore Christ is not man . . . A man led by God is not God, but a body joined to God is God. But Christ is God. Therefore he is not a man led by God but a body in composition with God . . . We acknowledge that the same one is Son of God and God according to the spirit, and son of man according to the flesh. The one Son is not two natures, the one to be adored, the other not to be adored; but one nature of the Word of God, made flesh, and to be adored with that flesh by one adoration.

(ed. Lietzmann 242-244)

Commentary: The phrase "One nature of the Word of God, made flesh" is a celebrated one, for it was taken over by Cyril of Alexandria on the mistaken assumption that it belonged to Athanasius, and was a bone of contention in the Nestorian controversy. Cyril's understanding of it was, however, different from that of Apollinarius, as we shall see.

The Incarnation of the Word of God

Not two sons, the one the Son of God, true God, to be adored, the other a man from Mary, not to be adored, become son of God by grace, as men do. But, as I said, the one Son of God who is from God and is God: him and no other, born of Mary according to the flesh in the last days.

The one who was born of the virgin Mary, Son of God and true God by nature and not by grace and not by participation, a man only according to the flesh which he received from Mary; according to the spirit he is Son of God and true God, suffering our sufferings according to the flesh . . . but remaining impassible and unchangeable according to his divinity . . .

If anyone should teach anything different against these sayings from holy scripture, saying that the Son of God is not the same as the son of Mary, the man adopted by grace like us; so as to make two sons, one by nature the Son of God, the other by grace, the man born of Mary; or if anyone says that the flesh of our Lord is from above and not from the virgin Mary, or that the Godhead was turned into flesh or mixed with it or changed, or that the Godhead of the Lord suffered, or that the flesh of our Lord is not to be adored since it is of a man, and not to be adored as the flesh of our Lord and God, that man is anathematized by the Catholic Church . . . (ed. Lietzmann 250-53)

3. GREGORY OF NAZIANZUS

Introduction

Gregory of Nazianzus (d. 389) and the two brothers Basil of Caesarea and Gregory of Nyssa, form perhaps the most famous trio in the history of theology, and are known as the Cappadocians. They played a leading role in developing trinitarian doctrine and terminology towards the end of the disputes arising after the Council of Nicaea. They also contributed much to the refutation of Apollinarianism, and Gregory of Nazianzus' letters to Cledonius, especially the first, are a masterly defense, based especially on soteriological grounds, of the human mind of Christ.

Letter 101 (First to Cledonius)

If anyone has put his trust in him [Christ] as a man without a human mind, he is really bereft of mind, and quite unworthy of salvation. For that which he has not assumed he has not healed, but that which is united to his Godhead is also saved.

Commentary: This is Gregory's famous formulation of the soteriological principle employed by the fathers against various heresies. In the entire passage he is concerned to show the threat to our salvation in the Apollinarian denial of a human mind in Christ.

If only half Adam fell, then that which Christ assumes and saves may be half also; but if the whole of his nature fell, it must be united to the whole nature of him that was begotten, and so be saved as a whole. Let them not, then, begrudge us our complete salvation, or clothe the savior only with bones and nerves and the portraiture of humanity. For if his manhood is without soul, even the Arians admit this, that they may attribute his passion to the Godhead, as that which gives motion to the body is also that which suffers. But if he has a soul, and yet is without a mind, how is he man? For man is not a mindless animal. And this would necessarily involve that while his form and tabernacle was human, his soul should be that of a horse or an ox, or some other of the brute creation. This, then, would be what he saves; and I have been deceived by the truth, and led to boast of an honor which has been bestowed upon another. But if his manhood is intellectual and not without mind, let them cease to be thus really mindless.

But, says such a one, the Godhead took the place of the human intellect. How does this touch me? For Godhead joined to flesh alone is not man, nor to soul alone, nor to both apart from intellect, which is the most essential part of man. Keep, then, the whole man, and mingle Godhead therewith, that you may benefit me in my completeness . . .

But, it may be said, our mind is subject to condemnation. What, then, of our flesh? Is that not subject to condemnation? You must therefore either set aside the latter on account of sin, or admit the former on account of salvation. If he assumed the worse that he might sanctify it by his incarnation, may he not assume the better that it may be sanctified by his becoming man? If the clay was leavened and has become a new lump, O you wise men, shall not the image be leavened and mingled with God, being deified by his Godhead?

Commentary: Gregory here employs an *a fortiori* argument, showing that the soul, the image of God, had a greater claim to divinization than the body.

And I will add this also: If the mind was utterly rejected, as prone to sin and subject to damnation, and for this reason he assumed a body but left out the mind, then there is an excuse for them who sin with the mind; for the witness of God—according to you—has shown the impossibility of healing it. Let me state the greater results. You, my good sir, dishonor my mind (you a sarcolater [adorer of flesh] if I am an anthropolater [adorer of man]) that you may tie God down to the flesh, since he cannot be otherwise tied; and therefore you take away the wall of partition. But what is my theory, who am but an ignorant man, and no philosopher? Mind is mingled with mind, as nearer and more closely related, and through it with flesh, being a mediator between God and carnality.

Commentary: Here we have again Origen's idea of the mind of Christ as mediating the union of flesh with the Word. The idea has become a commonplace in theology through the formula, "The body is assumed through the mediation of the soul."

Further let us see what is their account of the assumption of manhood, or the assumption of flesh, as they call it. If it was in order that God, otherwise incomprehensible, might be comprehended, and might converse with men through his flesh as through a veil, their mask and the drama which they represent is a pretty one, not to say that it was open to him to converse with us in other ways, as of old, in the burning bush and in the appearance of a man. But if it was that he might destroy the condemnation by sanctifying like by like, then as he needed flesh for the sake of the flesh which had incurred condemnation, and soul for the sake of our soul, so, too, he needed mind for the sake of mind, which not only fell in Adam, but was the first to be affected, as the doctors say of illnesses.

Commentary: Implicit in this idea of sanctifying like by like is the conception of physico-mystical redemption entertained especially by the Greek Fathers. It is due in part to their Platonism, but also has roots in scripture (e.g., Hebrews 2:11). Gregory here bases his argument on a threefold division of man.

For that which received the command was that which failed to keep the command, and that which failed to keep it was that also which dared to transgress; and that which transgressed was that which stood most in need of salvation; and that which needed salvation was that which also he took upon him. Therefore, mind was taken upon him. (LCC 4.218-21)

Second Oration on Easter 22

To whom and for what reason was the great and famous blood of our high-priest and victim poured out? We were, of course, held by the evil one and sold under sin and had exchanged virtue for pleasure. Now if ransom is paid to no one but the captor, I ask to whom it was offered and for what reason? If to the evil one, what a shame! If not only something from God but God himself is taken by the robber as ransom and so precious a price is paid to his tyranny, what reason could there have been for showing us mercy? But if it was paid to the Father—first of all, how? For we were not held in his power. Secondly, what reason would there be that the blood of the only-begotten would please the Father? He did not even receive the sacrifice of Isaac by his father but changed the sacrifice by having a lamb substituted for the rational victim. Is it not rather clear that the Father accepted the offering, not that he asked for it or needed it, but because of his divine plan and because man had to be sanctified by the humanity of God, so that he might deliver us by overcoming forcibly the power of the tyrant and bring us to himself through his Son who is the mediator and who works out everything to the honor of the Father? (PG 36.653)

Commentary: Here Gregory criticizes the so-called "ransom" theory of redemption, found in many of the fathers, including his friend Gregory of Nyssa. This theory takes too literally the metaphorical language of scripture when it speaks of the payment of the blood of Christ on our behalf. Nazianzen here exposes the absurdity of a true ransom paid either to the devil or to God. Not till St. Anselm in the eleventh century will the literalism be surmounted.

4. GREGORY OF NYSSA

Introduction

Gregory of Nyssa (d. 394) was the speculative giant among the Cappadocians, and, with Athanasius, perhaps the foremost exponent of the physico-mystical conception of redemption. As a Platonist he had a strong conviction of the organic unity of mankind, and this gave him a suitable speculative apparatus with which to develop the Pauline doctrine of our common fall in Adam and common redemption in Christ. His Christology leans more towards Antioch than towards Alexandria, for he stresses the duality present in Christ. However, like Origen he speaks of the risen Christ in such a way that there appears to be no persevering role for his humanity; it is totally transformed into divinity, like a drop of vinegar in the ocean. As we said in the case of Origen, the import of such statements is not ontological but mystical. Like Origen, Gregory is much influenced in his Christology by his deep concern for the mystical life of the Christian, of which Christ is the model.

Address on Religious Instruction 16

When, in his case too, soul and body had been separated by that successive moment of change our nature undergoes, he joined the parts together again with a kind of glue—I mean by divine power. And so he united what was separated in an unbreakable union. This is what the resurrection means—the restoration of elements into an indissoluble union after their separation, so that they can grow together. In this way man's primal grace was restored and we retrieved once more eternal life . . . Now just as the principle of death had its origin in a single person and passed to the whole of human nature, similarly the principle of the resurrection originated in one man and extends to all humanity . . . For when in the case of the man in whom he was incarnate the soul returned once more to the body after the dissolution, a similar union of the separated elements potentially passed to the whole of human nature, as if a new beginning had been made. This is the mystery of God's plan with regard to death, and of the resurrection from the dead. He does not prevent the soul's separation from the body by death in accordance with the inevitable course of nature. But he brings them together again by the resurrection. Thus he becomes the meeting point of both, of death and of life. In himself he restores the nature which death has disrupted, and becomes himself the principle whereby the separated parts are reunited. (LCC 3.294-95)

Commentary: Gregory of Nyssa here expresses the physico-mystical conception of redemption, with stress on the idea that solidarity between Christ and the rest of mankind required that his death and resurrection might be the restoration to life of all men. This solidarity is frequently referred to technically as "inclusion," and, as in other Greek fathers, Gregory's Platonism assists him in conceiving how all men are in a sense one man. He is, of course, echoing St. Paul's teaching on the first and second Adam (cf. Rom 5:12-21).

Address on Religious Instruction 23-24

How can we recount in detail each of the gospel miracles? When the enemy saw such power, he recognized in Christ a bargain which offered him more than he held. For this reason he chose him as the ransom for those he had shut up in death's prison. Since, however, he could not look upon the direct vision of God, he had to see him clothed in some part of that flesh which he already held captive through sin. Consequently the deity was veiled in flesh, so that the enemy, by seeing something familiar and natural to him, might not be terrified at the approach of transcendent power. So when he saw this power softly reflected more and more through the miracles, he reckoned that what he saw was to be desired rather than feared. You observe here how goodness is combined with justice, and wisdom is not separated from them. Through the covering of the flesh the divine power is made accessible, so that the enemy will not take fright at God's appearing and so thwart his plan for us. All God's attributes are at once displayed in this—his goodness, his wisdom, and his justice. That he decided to save us is proof of his goodness. That he struck a bargain to redeem the captive indicates his justice. And it is evidence of his transcendent wisdom that he contrived to make accessible to the enemy what was [otherwise] inaccessible . . . God's transcendent power is not so much displayed in the vastness of the heavens, or the luster of the stars, or the orderly arrangement of the universe or his perpetual oversight of it, as in his condescension to our weak nature. We marvel at the way the sublime entered a state of lowliness and, while actually seen in it, did not leave the heights. We marvel at the way the Godhead was entwined in human nature and, while becoming man, did not cease to be God. As we have already observed, the opposing power could not, by its nature, come into immediate contact with God's presence and endure the unveiled sight of him. Hence it was that God, in order to make himself easily accessible to him who sought the ransom for us, veiled himself in our nature. In that way, as it is with greedy fish, he might swallow the Godhead like a fishhook along with the flesh, which was the bait. Thus, when life came to dwell with death and light shone upon darkness, their contraries might vanish away. For it is not in the nature of darkness to endure the presence of light, nor can death exist where life is active. (LCC 3.300-301)

Commentary: Though Gregory is, as we have seen, one of the foremost exponents of the physico-mystical conception of redemption, this did not prevent him from conceiving redemption as also a process of liberation from the power of Satan. To this end he employs the famous image of the bargain struck between God and Satan. The latter is conceived to have certain rights over sinful mankind, which God binds himself to respect, so that the devil must receive his due in the manner in which man is rescued from his grasp. This is brought about by a divine deception: the flesh of Christ veiling his divinity was a kind of bait attractive to the devil. In seizing at the humanity by inflicting death on Christ, he was hooked by the hidden divinity of the God-man. Today we think of Gregory as taking too literally the biblical metaphors; but perhaps it is we who are taking Gregory's description in this catechetical work more seriously than he intended.

Address on Religious Instruction 32

What further objection do our opponents bring forward? In its extreme form this: that the transcendent nature ought never to have experienced death. Rather could he, with his excessive power, have easily accomplished his purpose without this. But even if, for some ineffable reason, this actually had to happen, he at least did not have to be humiliated by a shameful manner of death. For, they urge, what death could be more shameful than that on a cross? What do we reply to this? That the birth makes the death necessary. He who had once decided to share our humanity had to experience all that belongs to our nature. Now human life is encompassed within two limits, and if he had passed through one and not touched the other, he would only have half fulfilled his purpose, having failed to reach the other limit proper to our nature. But someone, perhaps, with an accurate grasp of our religion might more reasonably claim that the death did not occur because of the birth, but that, on the contrary, the birth was accepted by him for the sake of the death. For he who eternally exists did not submit to being born in a body because *he* was in need of life. Rather was it to recall *us* from death to life. Our whole nature had to be brought back from death. In consequence he stooped down to our dead body and stretched out a hand, as it were, to one who was prostrate. He approached so near death as to come into contact with it, and by means of his own body to grant our nature the principle of the resurrection, by raising our total humanity along with him by his power. Not from another source, but from the lump of our humanity, came the manhood which received the divine. By the resurrection it was exalted along with the Godhead. In the case of our own bodies the activity of one of our senses is felt throughout the whole system which is united to it. In just the same way, seeing that our nature constitutes, as it were, a single living organism, the resurrection of one part of it extends to the whole. By the unity and continuity of our nature it is communicated from the part to the whole. If, then, he who stands upright stoops to raise up one who has fallen, what is there in our religious teaching which is outside the realm of probability? (LCC 3.309-10)

Commentary: Gregory here returns to the physico-mystical conception of redemption. Human nature is seen as constituting a single organism, so that the resurrection of one is the resurrection of all. It was thus important that the humanity of Christ should be physically derived from our race. Gregory also reflects on the relationship between the human birth of Christ and his human death. Once born of mankind, the Word had to go all the way and accept human death. More profoundly, his birth was ordered to his death, for it was precisely his death, not his birth, which was required to rescue us from death.

5. CYRIL OF JERUSALEM

Introduction

Cyril of Jerusalem (d. 386), though a strong defender of Christ's divinity against Arianism, was not very prominent in the fourth-century Christological disputes. Some excerpts from his catechetical sermons will be helpful, however, in illustrating just how catechumens of the period were instructed on the incarnation.

Catechetical Lectures 4.9

You must believe that this only-begotten Son of God came down from heaven to this earth because of our sins, and took upon him manhood of like passions with ours, by being born of the holy virgin and of Holy Spirit, and this incarnation was not docetic or imaginary, but true incarnation. He did not pass through the virgin as though passing through a channel, but his flesh grew truly from her flesh and he was truly fed upon her milk. He truly ate as we eat, and drank as we drink. For if the incarnation was but seeming, then did it but seem to bring salvation. (LCC 4.103-4)

Commentary: Here Cyril repeats against docetism the soteriological argument we have seen in patristic tradition from Ignatius of Antioch onwards.

Catechetical Lectures 10.3-5

You are to believe "in one Lord Jesus Christ, the only-begotten Son of God." We say "one" Lord Jesus Christ to show that his sonship is unique. We say "one" to stop anyone dreaming that there could be another. We say "one" lest you should hear of his work under manifold means and fall into the blasphemous notion that it is the work of a plurality of sons. For he is called a *door.* But you must not think of a wooden door. You must think of a spiritual door that reasons and is alive, and knows all about those that enter. He has the title *way,* not as if he were trodden by our feet, but as bearing us on our way to our Father in the heavens. He is called *sheep,* not as if he were an animal, but to express the fact that he cleanses the whole world of sins by his precious blood, that he was led "before his shearer" and knew when was the time to be "dumb" [cf. Is 53:7]. This sheep is equally called *shepherd,* and says "I am the good shepherd" [Jn 10:11]. By his manhood he is sheep, by his divine loving-kindness he is shepherd. Do you want to be assured that there are human sheep? The savior tells the apostles, "Behold I send you as sheep in the midst of wolves" [Mt 10:16]. He is called, again, *lion;* not of the man-eating kind, but to point out, as it were, by this name, how royal, immovable, and boldly confident is his nature. He is called lion also as opposing the lion that we are afraid of, that roars and then swallows up such as are taken in. For the savior came to tread down our adversary and rescue those that put their trust in him, not as if he put aside the gentleness that is his by nature, but as the strong "lion of the tribe of Judah" [Apoc 5:5]. And he is called a *stone,* not such an inanimate stone as is quarried by the hands of men, but such a "chief corner-stone" that "whosoever believeth in him shall not be ashamed" [Is 28:16].

He is called *Christ,* not for any unction from human hands, but from the Father's, as having been anointed for eternal high-priesthood on behalf of men.

Commentary: The Greek name or title "Christ," like the Hebrew "messiah" means "anointed." Cyril here brings out what later theology will call the substantial anointing of Christ in his humanity by the very fact of the incarnation.

He is called the *dead,* not as having gone to "join the majority" like all souls in Hades, but as the one "free among the dead." He is called *son of man,* not as it is said of each one of us that we sprang from earth, but in the context of his "coming in the clouds of heaven" [Dn 7:13] to judge both the quick and the dead. He is called *Lord,* not in the catachrestic [improper] sense in which the title is given to men, but as possessing lordship by right of nature and forever. He is called *Jesus* [savior] because the name fits him, and he has that appellation in view of the saving medicine he brings. He is called *Son,* not meaning that God promoted him to that dignity, but that he was naturally begotten as Son. Many indeed are the names of our savior. And so, lest the plurality of names should suggest to you a plurality of sons, and in view of the heretical error according to which Christ and Jesus are not one and the same, with the door likewise and all the other names, the faith keeps you out of danger by saying "In one Lord Jesus Christ": for though the names are many, their bearer is one.

Commentary: Cyril is here cautioning his converts against those Christologies stemming from Paul of Samosata which so divide divinity and humanity in Christ as to speak of two sons (a view which we shall see shortly in Diodore of Tarsus). Note Cyril's use of "one and the same," a key phrase which we have seen in Irenaeus, and shall see in the definition of Chalcedon.

It is for the good of each individual that the savior comes in many characters. For to those who need cheering, he proposes himself as *vine,* while he stands as *door* before those who should be entering. He stands before those who have prayers to pray, as their mediating *high priest.* He is *sheep,* again, to those with sins upon them, to be slain for those sins. He "becomes all things to all men" [1 Cor 9:22], and yet never changes from what he is in his own proper nature. For he goes on possessing the dignity of sonship that truly resists all change, and at the same time adapts himself to our infirmities as, shall we say, the very kindest of *physicians* or as an understanding *teacher.* He really is *Lord,* not as having step by step attained to lordship, but as having by nature the dignity of being Lord. He is not called Lord by courtesy as we are, but as being Lord in sheer fact, since he bears sway over all that he has himself created, and the Father wills it so. For if we bear sway, it is over men of equal status and like passions with ourselves, and often over our seniors; and very often a young master rules over old servants. But the lordship of our Lord Jesus Christ is not like that, but he is *Maker* first and Lord second. First he made all things by the Father's will, and thereafter is Lord of all he made. (LCC 4.131-34)

B. The West before Ephesus

1. POPE DAMASUS

Introduction

Pope Damasus played an important role in combating Apollinarianism. At the same time he made it clear that the opposite error, adoptionism, was unacceptable. Besides several letters sent by him to the East prior to the second ecumenical council at Constantinople in 381, we have the so-called *Tome of Damasus,* representing the action of a Roman synod in 382, just after Apollinarianism had been condemned by the council. The excerpts below give us a good view of the attitude of Rome toward the Christological disputes then raging in the East.

Letter to Eastern Bishops

We are amazed that some of our own, although they seem to have a holy understanding of the Trinity, are ignorant of the power of the scriptures and entertain wrong notions in the matter of the mystery of our salvation. They are said to say that our Lord and savior assumed an imperfect man from the virgin Mary, that is, one without a mind. How close they are to the Arians! The Arians say that the Godhead is imperfect in the Son of God; these wrongly say that the manhood is imperfect in the son of man. Surely if an imperfect humanity was assumed, God's gift is imperfect, our salvation is imperfect, because the whole man is not saved. And what will become of our Lord's words: "The son of man has come to save what was lost" [Mt 18:11]? The whole man, that is, in soul and body and mind and the complete nature of his being. If the whole man was lost, it was necessary that what was lost be saved; but if he is saved without his mind, it will be found that, contrary to the gospel, all that was lost has not been saved . . . What of the fact that the malice of original sin and the whole of damnation was in the mind? If the mind of man for choosing good and evil had not been lost he would not have died; how then could one maintain that the first part to sin did not need salvation? We who know that we have been wholly and completely saved profess that perfect God assumed perfect man. And so see to it that by their understanding of sound doctrine the minds of these men be saved who up to now did not believe that the mind was saved. (DS 146)

Commentary: In language very like that of Gregory of Nazianzus, Pope Damasus here argues that if Christ were without a human mind or spiritual soul, the more important part of man would be unredeemed. Note such phrases as "perfect God assumed perfect man." This is an example of the concrete *assumptus homo* ("assumed man") terminology. It was favored by the West and by Antioch, though we find it occasionally also in Alexandrian Christology. It has the advantage of bringing out that Christ was fully man, and also of suggesting the inclusion of all men in Christ in virtue of our common humanity. But it also has the disadvantage, if taken literally, of implying that a human person has been assumed. And so, from the time of St. Thomas on, Catholic theologians have usually preferred to speak of the assumption of a humanity or human nature rather than of the assumption of a man.

Tome of Damasus 5-7

We anathematize Photinus who has revived the Ebionite heresy by saying that the Lord Jesus Christ is only of Mary.

Commentary: Photinus, a disciple of Marcellus of Ancyra, was in the adoptionist tradition of Paul of Samosata. The Ebionites were an early Judaeo-Christian sect which denied the divinity of Jesus. Damasus is here insisting on the unity of Christ.

We anathematize those who say there are two sons, one before the ages, the other after the assumption of flesh from the virgin.

Commentary: This anathema is also directed against an adoptionist division of Christ. Diodore of Tarsus was a contemporary who held that there were two sons in Christ.

We anathematize those who say that the Word of God took the place in human flesh of the rational and intelligible soul, because the Son and Word of God was not in a body in place of a rational and intelligible soul, but rather assumed our soul, that is, a rational and intelligible one, and saved it. (DS 157-9)

Commentary: Here the position of the Arians and Apollinarians is condemned, with a brief indication of the soteriological principle now so familiar to us.

2. HILARY OF POITIERS

Introduction

Hilary (d. 367) united in his doctrine both western and eastern traditions. His conflict with the Arians is of central importance in his Christology, especially in his work on the Trinity. Against the Arian argument that since Christ had weaknesses and limitations he could not be God equal to the Father, Hilary—while making more positive mention of the human soul of Christ than did Athanasius—was nevertheless too inclined to withdraw the humanity from natural suffering, dependence on food and drink, and so forth. In addition, he conceives of the humanity as wholly divinized after the resurrection. Positively, it may be said that he maintains orthodoxy by distinguishing two natures in the one Christ. Also, he expresses the physico-mystical conception of our salvation: Christ's taking of flesh is the sanctification and renewal of the flesh of all of us.

The Trinity 2.24-5

In what remains we have the appointment of the Father's will. The virgin, the birth, the body, then the cross, the death, the visit to the lower world: these things are our salvation. For the sake of mankind the Son of God was born of the virgin and of the Holy Spirit. In this process he ministered to himself; by his own power—the power of God—which overshadowed her, he sowed the beginning of his body, and entered on the first stage of his life in the flesh. He did it so that by his incarnation he might take to himself from the virgin the fleshly nature, and that through this commingling there might come into being a hallowed body of all humanity; so that through that body which he was pleased to assume, all mankind might be hid in him, and he in return, through his unseen existence, be reproduced in all. Thus the invisible image of God scorned not the shame which marks the beginnings of human life. He passed through every stage: through conception, birth, wailing, cradle and every successive humiliation.

What worthy return can we make for so great a condescension? The only-begotten God, ineffably born of God, entered the virgin's womb and grew and took the frame of poor humanity. He who upholds the universe, within whom and through whom are all things, was brought forth by common childbirth; he at whose voice archangels and angels tremble, and heaven and earth and all the elements of this world are melted, was heard in childish wailing. The invisible and incomprehensible, whom sight and feeling and touch cannot gauge, was wrapped in a cradle. If any man thinks all this unworthy of God, the more must he admit his debt for the benefit conferred, the less such condescension befits the majesty of God. He by whom man was made had nothing to gain by becoming man; it was our gain that God was incarnate and dwelt among us, making all flesh his home by taking upon him the flesh of one. We were raised because he was lowered; shame to him was glory to us. He, being God, made flesh his residence, and we in return are lifted anew from the flesh to God. (based on NPNF 9.58-9)

Commentary: Here we have an example in Latin Christology of the physico-mystical conception of redemption.

The Trinity 10.23

The man Jesus Christ, only-begotten God, as flesh and as Word, at the same time son of man and Son of God, without ceasing to be himself, that is, God, took true humanity after the likeness of our humanity. But when, in this humanity, he was struck with blows, or smitten with wounds, or bound with ropes, or lifted on high, he felt the force of suffering, but without its pain. Thus a dart passing through water, or piercing a flame, or wounding the air, inflicts all that it by nature can: it passes through, it pierces, it wounds; but all this is without effect on the thing it strikes; since it is against the order of nature to make a hole in water, or pierce flame, or wound the air, though it is the nature of a dart to make holes, to pierce and to wound. So our Lord Jesus Christ suffered blows, hanging, crucifixion and death: but the suffering which attacked the body of the Lord, without ceasing to be suffering, had not the natural effect of suffering. It exercised its function of punishment with all its violence; but the body of Christ by its virtue suffered the violence of the punishment without consciousness of it. True, the body of the Lord would have been capable of feeling pain like our natures, if our bodies possessed the power of treading on the waters and walking over the waves without weighing them down by our tread or forcing them apart by the pressure of our steps, if we could pass through solid substances, and the barred doors were no obstacle to us. But, as only the body of our Lord could be borne up by the power of his soul in the waters, could walk upon the waves, and pass through walls, how can we judge of the flesh conceived of the Holy Spirit on the analogy of a human body? That flesh, that is, that bread, is from heaven; that humanity is from God. He had a body to suffer, and he suffered: but he had not a nature which could feel pain. For his body possessed a unique nature of its own; it was transformed into heavenly glory on the mount, it put fevers to flight by its touch, it gave new eyesight by its spittle.

(based on NPNF 9.187-8)

Commentary: This is one passage in which Hilary, trying to meet the Arian argument, is forced to weaken Christ's likeness to us.

The Trinity 10.55

Again, how great a mystery of word and act it is that Christ wept, that his eyes filled with tears from the anguish of his mind [Lk 19:41]. Whence came this defect in his soul that sorrow should wring tears from his body? What bitter fate, what unendurable pain, could move to a flood of tears the son of man who descended from heaven? Again, what was it in him which wept? God the Word, or his human soul? For though weeping is a bodily function, the body is but a servant; tears are, as it were, the sweat of the agonized soul. Again, what was the cause of his weeping? Did he owe to Jerusalem the debt of tears, Jerusalem, the godless parricide, whom no suffering could requite for the slaughter of apostles and prophets, and the murder of her Lord himself? He might weep for the disaster and death which befall mankind: but could he grieve for the fall of that doomed and desperate race? What, I ask, was this mystery of weeping? His soul wept for sorrow: was not it the soul which sent forth the prophets? Which would so often have gathered the chickens together under the shadow of his wings [cf. Mt 23:37; Lk 13:34]? But God the Word cannot grieve, nor can the Spirit weep: nor could his soul possibly do anything before the body existed. Yet we cannot doubt that Jesus Christ truly wept. (NPNF 9.197)

Commentary: Hilary here seems to be intensely aware of the mystery involved in the human tears of a divine person!

Treatise on the Psalms 53.7

The only-begotten Son of God, the Word of God and God the Word . . . in order to be the most absolute example for us of human lowliness asked for and suffered everything human. And he asked to be delivered from our common weakness, that it might be understood that he had our human origin with the burden of our weakness. That is why he was hungry, thirsty; he slept, was tired out, had to run away from an irreligious mob, was sad, wept and suffered and died. And that it might be understood that he was subject to all this not by nature but by taking it upon himself, when he had experienced all these things he rose from the dead.

(CSEL 22.140)

Commentary: Though the commentaries on the psalms, written some years after the work on the Trinity, emphasize a little more the reality of the sufferings of Christ, Hilary insists that the suffering was not natural but freely chosen.

On the Psalms 68.25

Coming in the form of a servant he emptied himself of the form of God. For who could exist in the form of man while remaining in the form of God? The form of God could not be done away with so that only the form of man would remain. He is both stripping himself of the form of God and assuming the form of man, because neither is the emptying of the form of God an extinction of his heavenly nature nor is the assumption of the form of a servant anything like a genuine origin and original state of being, because what is assumed is not his inmost self but an external acquisition. (CSEL 22.334)

Commentary: Hilary places great emphasis on the *kenosis* (the self-emptying) of the Word in the incarnation (cf. Phil 2:7). It has in fact been asked whether he fell into kenotic doctrine, according to which the divine nature disappeared in the taking of a human nature. The present passage shows that Hilary understands the kenosis as touching the self-manifestation, not the basic constitution, of the Word in his lowly human state.

3. JEROME

Introduction

Though Jerome (d. 419) had no great direct influence on the progress of Christology, he does present us with an interesting example of western Christology—deriving much, however, from such giants of the East as Origen. He stresses the duality of natures in Christ, and insists on the human feelings and sufferings of the savior. We should recall that he spent more than three decades at the end of his life at Bethlehem, absorbed in literary labors, correspondence, and contemplation. This milieu is undoubtedly responsible for the deep personal devotion to Christ which shines out often in his sermons.

Commentary on Matthew 2.14

The fact that he went up alone to pray, we should refer not to him who from five loaves filled five thousand people, not counting women and children, but to him who, when he heard of John's death, went out into the desert. Not that we divide the personality of the Lord but that his actions were sometimes divine, sometimes human. (PL 26.105)

Commentary on Matthew 4.26

"He began to grow sorrowful and be sad" [Mt 26:37]. What we said previously about passion and "propassion" ["the difference between passion and propassion is this, that passion is reckoned a vice whereas propassion, although it is deplorable as the beginning of wrong, nevertheless is not culpable" 1. 5. 28 (PL 26.39)] is clear also in the present chapter. The Lord, to show the reality of the man he had assumed, really became sorrowful; but he did it through "propassion" so that a passion would not dominate his soul. It is one thing to be sorrowful; it is another to begin to be sorrowful. He was becoming sorrowful not from fear of suffering, because he had come for that and he had rebuked Peter foı his timidity, but because of the unhappy Judas . . . But if the heretics wish to interpret the savior's sadness of soul not as his feelings towards those being lost but as a passion, let them tell us how they interpret what Ezekiel puts in the mouth of God [Ezech 16:43 (LXX)]: "And in all these things you made me sorrowful." (PL 26.205)

Commentary: Like Hilary before him, Jerome here faces the dilemma of reconciling the utter sinlessness of Christ with the fullness of his human life. He offers a solution more satisfactory than that of Hilary in that suffering is natural to Christ in his humanity. The distinction between passion and "propassion" he derives from the tradition of Origen; it occurs in a commentary on the psalms discovered at Tours in 1941 (cf. Grillmeier 273-75 and 314-15). See also below the passage from Jerome's treatment of Psalm 108.

Letter 120 to Hedibia

The glory of the savior is the gibbet on which he triumphed. He is crucified as man, glorified as God. We say this, not that we believe that one is God and the other man, so as to make two persons in the one Son of God, as the new heresy falsely does. The Son of God and the son of man are one and the same and whatever is spoken of him is referred now to his divine glory, now to our salvation. (CSEL 55.497-8)

Homilies on the Psalms 108.31

If he had sadness, if he had grief, then he had feeling. If then they should wish to tell us, "We say that he did not have feeling in order that he might not seem to have sin," our answer to them is: Did he have a body like us or did he not? If they say, "He did," our answer to them is: Then he had the passions which our bodies have. Everyone understands what I am saying. If they should say that he did not have bodily passions or desires, we say to them: Then he did not have a body either. And we may say to them: Just as he had a true body like us without having the body's sin, so he had a true soul without having the soul's sin. Let us acknowledge, then, that he had a true body and a true soul. For if the Lord did not assume all that belongs to man, he did not save man. And if he assumed the body without assuming the soul, then he has saved the body, but has not saved the soul. But we maintain that our soul is saved more than our body. Hence the Lord assumed both body and soul, in order to save both, in order to save the complete man, even as he created him. (CCL 78.220-1)

Commentary: Here Jerome is even more insistent than in the *Commentary on Matthew* (see above) on the reality of suffering and emotion in Christ. Note his application of the soteriological principle: What has not been assumed has not been saved. In this connection it is interesting that Jerome had known Apollinarius personally.

Christmas Sermon

Now that we have spoken at length and seen and adored the infant crying in the manger, let us adore him even today. Let us take him in our arms, let us adore him, the Son of God. The great God who for so long thundered from heaven and did not save, cried and did save. Why do I say all this? Because pride never saves; humility saves. The Son of God was in heaven and was not adored; he comes down to earth and is adored. He had underneath him the sun and the moon and the angels and was not worshipped; he is born on earth a complete man, wholly man, to heal the world. Whatever of man he did not assume, he did not save; if he assumed a body and did not assume a soul, he did not save it. Did he then save the lesser part and not save the greater part?

(CCL 78.528-529)

Commentary: Here we find both Jerome the contemplative of Bethlehem and Jerome the theologian. The first several sentences sound much like Augustine, who also loves to stress in antithetical phrases the saving humility of the God-man. In the last few sentences Jerome repeats the familiar soteriological argument for the presence of a human mind in Christ.

4. AMBROSE

Introduction

Called to the episcopacy from the life of a government official, and primarily pastoral in outlook, Ambrose (d. 397) was no speculative theologian and made no major contribution to Christology. His defense of orthodoxy against Arianism and Apollinarianism is the context in which his doctrine on the person and work of Christ is formulated.

Letter 48.5

Let us acknowledge that just as in the form of God nothing was lacking of the divine nature and fullness, so in the form of man nothing was lacking to his being judged perfect man. He came to save the whole man. It was not right that he who achieved a perfect work in others should suffer imperfection in himself. If he were lacking anything he did not redeem everything. If he did not redeem everything he deceived us in saying that he was saving the whole man. But since it is impossible for God to lie [Heb 6:18], he did not deceive us. And so he who came to redeem and save the whole assumed everything that was part of human perfection. (PL 16.1202-3)

Commentary: Ambrose is here cautioning his correspondent against Apollinarianism, and employs the soteriological argument to establish the integrality of our Lord's humanity.

The Mystery of the Lord's Incarnation 7

"And Jesus grew in wisdom," etc. [Lk 2:52]. How did the wisdom of God grow? The sequence of the words can tell you. It was a growth in age and a growth in wisdom, but human wisdom. That is why he puts "age" first, so that you may realize he is speaking of him as man. Age does not belong to the divinity but to the body. Therefore if he grew in the age of a man, he was growing in the wisdom of a man. Wisdom grows by sense-experience because it develops out of sense-perception . . . His human sense-experience grew; therefore, he assumed human senses. (PL 16.872-3)

Commentary: Ambrose here answers the Arian objection that Jesus' growth in knowledge (cf. Lk 2:52) is proof that he is not God, by distinguishing between divinity and humanity. He elsewhere shows himself reluctant, however, to employ the same distinction where there is question of ignorance in Christ (cf. Mk 13:32).

Treatise Sent to Gratian Concerning Faith 7

As man he hesitates, as man he is troubled. His power is not troubled, his divinity is not troubled, but his soul is troubled, he is troubled in the human weakness he has taken on himself. And because he took our soul, he took the passions of the soul; for God, as God, could not be troubled or die . . . And so those words "the Lord was crucified" we understand to mean not that he was crucified in his glory, but because the same one is God and man—God in his divinity, the man Jesus Christ by assuming flesh—the Lord of glory is said to be crucified. (PL 16.594-5)

Commentary: Here too Ambrose meets the Arians by distinguishing humanity and divinity. At the same time he always insisted that Christ was one and the same, and he makes frequent use of the mutual predication of properties. He makes no effort to push further in understanding the mystery of unity and distinction in Christ. He is content to reject docetism, Arianism, and Apollinarianism.

5. AUGUSTINE

Introduction

Augustine died in 430. He had, therefore, no direct role in formulating the doctrine of the two great Christological councils. But his view of Christ is of special interest both because he weaves into it some of his central insights and themes, and because it was to have a large impact on the West. For him Christ is the mediator between God and man; the Word incarnate; the second Adam; the head of the Church, his body; the humble physician who comes to heal the ravages of sin and pride; the teacher par excellence, who gives to men the example of God's gracious charity and humility in taking mortal flesh; our wisdom and knowledge, leading us to eternity through the things of time; the model of our Christian life in that his grace and predestination as God's Son were unmerited.

The Christian Combat 11

Let the human race take hope and rediscover its own nature. Let it see what an important place it occupies among the works of God. Men! do not despise yourselves—the Son of God assumed manhood. Women! do not despise yourselves—the Son of God was born of a woman. Yet, do not love things carnal, for in the sight of the Son of God we are neither male nor female. Do not love things temporal; for if it were right to love them, the human nature assumed by the Son of God would have loved them. Do not be afraid of insults and crosses and death; for if these were harmful to man, the human nature assumed by the Son of God would not have suffered them . . . If we have a high opinion of ourselves, let us deign to imitate him who is called the Son of the Most High. If we have a lowly opinion of ourselves, let us presume to imitate the fishermen and publicans who imitated him.

Commentary: Augustine is frequently and with good reason taxed with pessimism, especially regarding original sin and marriage. In these lines we have an instance of his Christian optimism, which is an optimism of grace.

O medicine, making provision for all: deflating what is distended; renewing what is wasting away; cutting away what is superfluous; preserving what is necessary; restoring what has been lost; curing what is corrupted! Who will now raise himself up against the Son of God? Who can despair of his own salvation, for whom the Son of God has willed to become so lowly? Who can believe that happiness is to be found in those things which the Son of God has taught us to despise? What tribulation can overcome him who believes that in the Son of God human nature was preserved intact amid violent persecution? Who can imagine himself shut out from the kingdom of heaven when he knows that publicans and prostitutes have imitated the Son of God? What wickedness can be found in him who makes that man's deeds and words the object of his contemplation, love and striving, in whom the Son of God revealed himself to us as a pattern of life? (FC 2.329-30)

Commentary: Several Augustinian themes occur in this paragraph: 1. the healing role of Christ and his grace; 2. that man must use *(uti)* temporal things, but seek delight *(frui)* or happiness *(beatitudo)* only in God; 3. the imitation of Christ.

Letter 137

But there are some who request an explanation of how God is joined to man so as to become the single person of Christ, as if they themselves could explain something that happens every day, namely, how the soul is joined to the body so as to form the single person of a man. For as the soul makes use of the body in a single person to form a man, so God makes use of man in a single person to form Christ. In the former person there is a mingling [*mixtura*] of soul and body; in the latter person there is a mingling of God and man; but the hearer must abstract from the property of material substance by which two liquids are usually so mingled that neither retains its separate character, although, among such substances, light mingled with air remains unchanged. Therefore, the person of man is a mingling of soul and body, but the person of Christ is a mingling of God and man, for when the Word of God is joined to a soul which has a body, it takes on both the soul and the body at once. The one process happens daily in order to beget men; the other happened once to set men free. However, it ought to be easier to believe in the intermingling of two incorporeal things than of one incorporeal and the other corporeal. (FC 20.26-7)

Commentary: Here Augustine sets out from the mystery of the unity of soul and body in man to defend the mystery of the unity of divinity and humanity in Christ. He replies in the same fashion to Porphyry's objection to the incarnation, in *The City of God* 10.29 (CCL 47.305).

The Trinity 13.24

Now all this which the Word made flesh did and suffered for us in time and place, belongs, according to the distinction which we have undertaken to establish, to knowledge, not to wisdom. But because the Word is outside of time and place, he is co-eternal with the Father and everywhere present in his totality; if anyone can, and to the extent that he can, speak truly about this Word, his speech will belong to wisdom. And therefore the Word made flesh, which is Christ Jesus, possesses the treasures of wisdom and knowledge . . . If these two are distinguished from each other in that wisdom is attributed to what is divine and knowledge to what is human, I acknowledge, with all who believe in him, the presence of both in Christ . . . Therefore Christ is our knowledge, and likewise Christ is our wisdom. It is he who implants in us faith in things temporal, it is he who manifests to us the truth about things eternal. Through him we journey to him; we go through knowledge to wisdom, but without ever leaving one and the same Christ, "in whom are hidden all the treasures of wisdom and knowledge" [Col 2:3]. (PL 42.1033-4)

Commentary: Books 12-14 of *The Trinity* center about the distinction between knowledge *(scientia)* and wisdom *(sapientia).* Here knowledge has to do with the right use of the temporal, wisdom with the contemplation of the eternal. Knowledge is correlated with our life of faith (by which the mysteries of Christ in time serve as means to the eternal vision of God), wisdom with the heavenly vision. In Christ are all the treasures of both wisdom and knowledge, for he is both God and man. We go through knowledge to wisdom, through his humanity to his divinity, through the Word incarnate in time to the Word of eternity. It is this necessary mediation of the Word incarnate which drew Augustine back to the Christian faith of Monica; while neo-Platonism told him of the eternal Word, it did not tell him of the Word made flesh for our salvation.

Enchiridion 108

Certainly we would not be redeemed by the one mediator of God and man, the man Jesus Christ [1 Tim 2:5], if he were not also God. Now, when Adam was created, a righteous man to be sure, there was no need of a mediator. But once sin had created a wide rift between the human race and God, it was necessary that a mediator, who alone was born and lived and was put to death without sin, should reconcile us with God even to the extent of obtaining for us the resurrection of the body unto life everlasting, in order that the pride of man might be rebuked and cured through the humility of God; that man might be made to see how far he had departed from God, when the incarnate God came to summon him back; that man in his stubbornness might receive an example of obedience from the God-Man; that the fountain of grace might be opened by the only-begotten taking the form of a servant, a form which had no antecedent merits; that the resurrection also of the body, promised to the redeemed, might be presaged in the resurrection of the redeemer; that the devil might be conquered by that same nature which he rejoiced to have deceived, without man, however, taking glory in himself, lest pride spring up anew. And to this add whatever else those who are proficient in these matters can perceive and explain, or perceive without being able to explain, concerning the great mystery of the mediator. (ACW 3.102)

Commentary: From the viewpoint of mediation, Augustine here summarily presents the purpose of the incarnation under different aspects.

Predestination of the Saints 30-31

The most illustrious light of predestination and grace is the savior himself—the mediator himself between God and men, the man Christ Jesus. And, pray, by what preceding merits of its own, whether of works or of faith, did the human nature which is in him procure for itself that it should be this. Let this have an answer, I beg. The man, whence did he deserve this—to be assumed by the Word co-eternal with the Father into unity of person, and be the only-begotten Son of God? Was it because any kind of goodness in him preceded? What did he do before? What did he believe? What did he ask, that he should attain to this unspeakable excellence? Was it not by the act and the assumption of the Word that that man, from the time he began to be, began to be the only Son of God? Did not that woman full of grace conceive the only Son of God? Was he not born the only Son of God, of the Holy Spirit and the virgin Mary, not of the lust of the flesh, but by God's peculiar gift? Was it to be feared that as age matured this man, he would sin of free will? Or was the will in him not free on that account? And was it not so much the more free in proportion to the greater impossibility of his becoming the servant of sin? Certainly, in him human nature—that is to say, our nature—specially received all those specially admirable gifts, and any others that may most truly be said to be peculiar to him, by virtue of no preceding merits of its own . . . Therefore in him who is our head let there appear to be the very fountain of grace, whence, according to the measure of every man, he diffuses himself through all his members. It is by that grace that every man from the beginning of his faith becomes a Christian, by which grace that one man from his beginning became Christ . . . This, therefore, is the same predestination of the saints which most especially shone forth in the saint of saints; and who is there of these who rightly understand the declarations of the truth that can deny this predestination? . . . As, therefore, that one man was predestined to be our head, so we, being many, are predestined to be his members. Here let human merits which have perished through Adam keep silence, and let that grace of God reign which reigns through Jesus Christ our Lord, the only Son of God, the one Lord. Let whoever can find in our head the merits which preceded that peculiar generation, seek in us his members for those merits which preceded our manifold regeneration. (BWA 1.804-6)

Commentary: In this passage, the "doctor of grace" argues against Pelagianism by showing that grace and predestination are unmerited in us because even Christ did not merit his predestination and grace as natural Son of God.

C. The Nestorian and Monophysite Crises; Ephesus and Chalcedon

1. DIODORE OF TARSUS

Introduction

A champion of the divinity of Christ against Julian the Apostate, and a prominent anti-Apollinarian, Diodore (d. ca. 394) is generally looked on as a forerunner of the extreme Antiochene Christology of Theodore and Nestorius. He distinguishes the man born from Mary, who is son by grace, from God the Word who is Son by nature. But he also has some affinity with the Alexandrian school, in that he does not develop a theology of the human soul of Christ (for example, in explaining the growth of Christ in knowledge). His objection to Apollinarianism was concerned not with its truncating of Christ's humanity but with the threat it posed to the transcendence of the Word.

Syriac Fragments 27

If anyone wants improperly to call the Son of God, God the Word, the son of David because the temple of God is from David, let him do so. And let him call the one born from the seed of David Son of God by grace and not by nature: not forgetting the natural parents nor upsetting the order of things. Nor let him say that the incorporeal and eternal one is both from God and from David, is passible and impassible. (Xiberta 131-2)

Commentary: Here Diodore takes his position on the basic question: Are the son of Mary and the Son of God one and the same "he"? He answers substantially as Theodore and Nestorius will do, in the negative. Yet, as the following fragment shows, he is unwilling to speak of two sons.

Syriac Fragments 30

We do not say that there were two sons of one Father. God the Word is the only Son of God by nature, and he who is from Mary is by nature the son of David, by grace the Son of God. Let us admit this, however: The two are one Son; and let us place the impossibility in our terminology.

(Xiberta 132)

Syriac Fragments 31-2

The man born of Mary is son by grace; God the Word is Son by nature. Let a sonship, glory and immortality according to grace suffice for a body of our race and let not what has been made a temple of God the Word be raised above its nature. And let not God the Word be insulted instead of given due thanks. What insult is equal to putting him with a body and thinking he needs a body for perfect sonship?

(Xiberta 132)

Commentary: Diodore's concern for the transcendence of the Word here emerges. If the Word properly has the body as his own, how can he be divine? Arianism denied the divinity, arguing from the fact that the Word did have the body as his own. Diodore felt compelled to take just the opposite position.

Latin Fragments 1

"Jesus grew in age and wisdom" [Lk 2:52]. This cannot be said of the Word of God because he is perfect God born of a perfect one, wisdom from wisdom, power from power. He himself did not grow . . . What grew in wisdom and age was the flesh. As it was being fashioned and born, the divinity did not bestow all wisdom on it at once but shared it with the body little by little. (Xiberta 132)

Commentary: Diodore explains the growth of Christ in wisdom by attributing it to the flesh or body, without recourse to the human soul of the savior. In this he falls short of being fully Antiochene.

2. THEODORE OF MOPSUESTIA

Introduction

In Theodore, bishop of Mopsuestia (d. 428), Antiochene reaction against the Word-flesh Christology assumes a major voice. He is not a speculative theologian but the greatest Antiochene exegete and a pastor of souls. His Christology shows a twofold concern: first, to preserve the divine transcendence of the Word, which he sees compromised by Arianism and Apollinarianism in their denial of a human soul in Christ; and secondly, to find in the free but sinless human activity of the God-man, as manifested in the gospels, the agent and model of our liberation from sin and death. Unfortunately Theodore was without the necessary conceptual tools to achieve a fully balanced portrait of the savior. His consistent distinction of "the Word" from "the man assumed" by the Word was a distinction incompatible with the basic Christological revelation and with the implicit teaching of Nicaea. More than a century after his death, he and certain writings attributed to him were condemned by the Second Council of Constantinople (553). His orthodoxy is today a matter of extensive dispute.

Catechetical Homilies 5

The partisans of Arius and Eunomius, however, say that he assumed a body but not a soul, and that the nature of the Godhead took the place of the soul. They lowered the divine nature of the only-begotten to the extent that from the greatness of its nature it moved and performed the acts of the soul and imprisoned itself in the body and did everything for its sustenance. If the Godhead had replaced the soul he would not have been hungry or thirsty, nor would he have tired or been in need of food . . .

Commentary: We see here Theodore's concern for the Word's transcendence which would be compromised were he called upon to take the place of the human soul. Also, if it is the Godhead, not a human soul, which is the immediate principle of life, then its infinite perfection would exclude suffering from the body which it vitalizes.

If, however, divine nature was sufficient for all these things, human nature which was in need of the grace of salvation from God should not have been assumed, as according to the opinion of the heretics this same Godhead would have satisfied the requirements of human nature, and in this case it would have been superfluous to assume a body at all as the Godhead was able to perform all its acts. This, however, was not the will of God, who indeed wished to put on and raise the fallen man who is composed of a body and of an immortal and rational soul . . . As death was by man so also the resurrection from the dead [will be] by man . . . Therefore it was necessary that he should assume not only the body but also the immortal and rational soul; and not only the death of the body had to cease but also that of the soul, which is sin. Since according to the sentence of the blessed [Paul] sin entered the world through man, and death entered through sin, it was necessary that sin which was the cause of death should have first been abolished, and then the abolition of death would have followed by itself. If sin were not abolished we would have by necessity remained in mortality, and we would have sinned in our mutability; and when we sin, we are under punishment, and consequently the power of death will by necessity remain. (WS 5.55-9)

Commentary: Here Theodore presents the soteriological argument, and maintains that as death came to man only consequent upon sin, it is sin which must first be conquered by the assumption of a human soul.

Catechetical Homilies 8

It is obvious that they [our blessed fathers] do not teach that the divine nature of the only-begotten was born of a woman, as if it had its beginning in her, because they did not say that the one who was born of his Father before all the worlds and who is eternally from him and with him had his beginning from Mary, but they followed the sacred books which speak differently of natures while referring [them] to one *prosopon* on account of the close union that took place between them, so that they might not be believed that they were separating the perfect union between the one who was assumed and the one who assumed. If this union were destroyed, the one who was assumed would not be seen more than a mere man like ourselves. The sacred books refer the two Words [i.e., natures] as if to one Son, so that they might show in the same faith both the glory of the only-begotten and the honor of the man whom he assumed.

If each of them was Son and Lord by nature it would be possible for us to say two Sons and two Lords, according to the number of the persons, but one being Son and Lord by nature and the other being neither Son nor Lord by nature, we believe that the latter received these [attributes] through his close union with the only-begotten God the Word, and so we hold that there is one Son only; and we understand that the one who is truly Son and Lord is the one who possesses these [attributes] by nature, and we add in our thought the temple in which he dwells and in which he will always and inseparably remain on account of the inseparable union which he has with him and because of which we believe that he is both Son and Lord. (WS 5.90-1)

Commentary: Theodore is at great pains to avoid speaking of two Sons in Christ. In this case Jesus would be an adopted son, and a stronger case would be made for those who accused Theodore of an adoptionism like that of Paul of Samosata.

Catechetical Homilies 12

When this state of our affairs became desperate, our Lord God willed in his mercy to rectify it. With this end in view he assumed a man from us, who was a faithful keeper of all the divine commandments, and was found to be free from all sin with the exception of the punishment of death. The tyrant, however, who could do nothing else, brought an unjust death upon him at the hand of the Jews, his servants, but he willingly accepted it and sat in judgment with him before God, the just judge, who pronounced him not liable to the punishment of death which had been wickedly and unjustly brought upon him. And he became forever immune from death, and immortal and incorruptible by nature. And as such he ascended into heaven and became forever beyond the reach of the harm and injury of Satan, who was thus unable to do any harm to a man who was immortal, incorruptible and immutable, and who dwelt in heaven and possessed a close union with the divine nature. From the fact that the man who was assumed had such a confidence [with God], he became a messenger on behalf of all the [human] race so that the rest of mankind might participate with him in his great change . . . The benefits accruing to us are immutable and unchangeable, since Christ who died for us, and who rose from the dead and received close union with the divine nature, draws us, by his intercession for us, to the participation in resurrection and in the good things that emanate from it.

We draw nigh unto the sacrament [baptism] because we perform in it the symbols of the freedom from calamities from which we were unexpectedly delivered, and of our participation in these new and great benefits which originated in Christ our Lord. Indeed we expect to be partakers of these benefits which are higher than our nature, while even the possibility of their coming to us we had never expected.

(WS 6.22)

Commentary: This passage suggests Theodore's predominant view of the redemption. As sin and death came to all men through the free surrender of one man to Satan, so sin and death are overcome by one man's free conquest of Satan. Because of the perfect union between the "assumed man" and the Word, the man is perfectly sinless. Winning the verdict over Satan, who had unjustly inflicted death on him, he becomes immortal, and henceforth has the destiny of drawing men to participate, through baptism and the Christian life, in his freedom from sin and death.

On the Incarnation 15

When, therefore, they ask whether Mary is mother of the man or mother of God, let our reply be: Both. One in the very nature of things, the other by relation; mother of the man by nature, since it was a man who was in the womb of Mary and came forth from it; mother of God, because God was in the man whom she bore, not limited within him in nature, but existing in him by disposition of will.

(ed. Swete 2.310)

Commentary: Here again we see both the earnestness and the ultimate inadequacy of Theodore's effort to preserve the unity of Christ. He wishes somehow to preserve the traditional *theotokos* (mother of God); yet he understands the term in a weakened sense, because the man born from Mary is not identically God, but only has God (the Word) dwelling in him in a perfect union.

3. NESTORIUS

Introduction

Bishop of Constantinople from 428, Nestorius soon aroused opposition by his attack on the traditional Christological kerygma, especially the devotion to Mary as *theotokos* (mother of God). This brought him into conflict with Cyril of Alexandria, and after an exchange of letters and the efforts of both to enlist the support of Pope Celestine I, Nestorius was deposed by the Council of Ephesus in 431. He died in exile in the era of Chalcedon (451). Nestorius represented the Antiochene insistence on the transcendence of the Word and the integrality of Christ's humanity. In such expressions as "God has suffered," "God has been nursed at the breast," he saw a revival of Arianism and Apollinarianism. His own doctrine found the unity of Christ on the level of *prosopon* ("person"), which he understood not in the sense of the radical ontological subject, but rather of the self-manifestation which each nature makes. In Christ, the intimate union of two natures, each with its own "person," yields a third "person of union."

Second Letter to Cyril 2-7

In your superficial reading of the tradition from those holy men [the fathers of Nicaea (325)] you made an excusable mistake in thinking that they said that the Word, equally invisible with the Father, suffered; look more closely, if you will, to what they said and you will find that divine chorus of fathers did not say that the consubstantial divinity suffered nor that it was newly born, invisible as it is with the Father, nor that this Godhead rose since it was it which raised up the dissolved temple.

"I believe," they say, then, "in our Lord Jesus Christ, his only-begotten Son." You see how they first lay down as bases the names common to the Godhead and the manhood—Lord, Jesus, Christ, his only-begotten Son; then they build on that the tradition of his becoming man and resurrection and suffering. The result is that with these names, which designate what is common to both natures, the generation and the lordship of the Son are not separated, and yet what is proper to each nature is not endangered by a ruinous confusion.

Commentary: It is interesting to contrast the appeals to Nicaea and scripture made by Cyril and Nestorius. Cyril, using the mutual predication of properties, shows that Nicaea and scripture affirm both eternal birth and human activity of the same subject, the Son (Word). Nestorius on the other hand notes that these same sources use for the incarnation, passion, and so on, only names which are common to both natures. For example, it is not the Word who is said to suffer, but Jesus Christ. Along with his failure to distinguish abstract and concrete terms, Nestorius' preoccupation with how the one subject in Christ is named is perhaps his primary misconception in regard to verbal expression. It is understandable, since he lived at a time when orthodoxy was still groping for appropriate conceptual and linguistic tools.

Whenever the sacred scriptures speak of Our Lord's activity they never speak of the birth and suffering of the divinity but of the humanity of Christ. That is why the most accurate way of speaking of the holy virgin is "Christ-bearer," not "God-bearer." And listen to these words crying out to us from the gospel: "The book of the generation of Jesus Christ, the son of David, the son of Abraham" [Mt 1:1]. It is clear that God the Word was not the son of David. (ACO 1.1.1. 29-31)

Letter to Pope Celestine 2

We also have found no slight corruption of orthodoxy among some of those here, which we have treated with both sternness and gentleness [as demanded]. It is no small error, but similar to the corruption of Apollinarius and Arius, blending together the Lord's appearance as man into a kind of confused combination—so much so that certain of our clergy, some from inexperience, others from heretical error long kept concealed, as often happened even in the times of the apostles, err like heretics, and openly blaspheme God the Word consubstantial with the Father, as if he took his beginning from the Christ-bearing virgin, and grew up with his temple and was buried with [it] in the flesh; they even say that his flesh after the resurrection did not remain flesh, but was changed into the nature of Godhead. To speak briefly, they refer the Godhead of the only-begotten to the same origin as the flesh joined [with it], and kill it with the flesh, and blasphemously say that the flesh joined with the Godhead was turned into deity by the deifying Word, which is nothing more nor less than to corrupt both.

Commentary: Nestorius, who in coming to Constantinople as bishop had set himself the task of combating heresy, saw the errors of Apollinarius and Arius lurking in current Christology. Some of the positions he describes are truly heretical —e.g., that the flesh was changed after the resurrection into the nature of divinity. Note again that he does not distinguish between saying "God suffered," and "divinity suffered." Looking at Christ primarily from the viewpoint of nature, not of person or subject, he was prone to this fatal error.

They even dare to treat of the Christ-bearing virgin in a way as along with God, for they do not scruple to call her *theotokos,* when the holy and beyond-all-praise fathers at Nicaea said no more of the holy virgin than that our Lord Jesus Christ was incarnate of the Holy Spirit and the virgin Mary—not to mention the scriptures, which everywhere, both by angels and apostles, speak of the virgin as mother of Christ, not of God the Word . . . If anyone wishes to use this word *theotokos* with reference to the humanity which was born, joined to God the Word, and not with reference to the parent, we say that this word is not appropriate for her who gave birth, since a true mother should be of the same essence as what is born of her. But the term could be accepted in consideration of this, that the word is used of the virgin only because of the inseparable temple of God the Word which was of her, not because she is the mother of God the Word—for none gives birth to one older than herself. (LCC 3.347-8)

Commentary: Nestorius seems to have understood *theotokos* in an Arian and Apollinarian sense. What he failed to see was that *theotokos,* which had now become established in the Church's kerygma, contained a valid and necessary insight into the *unity* of divinity and humanity in Christ, and could be understood in an orthodox sense. He is, however, willing to accept the expression in a broad or improper sense.

4. CYRIL OF ALEXANDRIA AND THE COUNCIL OF EPHESUS

Introduction

Cyril, bishop of Alexandria (d. 444), brings the Word-flesh Christology to its peak influence in the Nestorian controversy, where he is the great champion of the unity of person in Christ and of the *theotokos* (mother of God). As with the fathers generally, his Christological position was largely dictated by pastoral concerns. He desired the most intimate possible union between the Word and human flesh because only thus could that flesh become the life-giving *organon* (instrument) of the Word in our divinization, especially in the eucharist. He is thus one of the foremost representatives of the physico-mystical idea of redemption.

Commentary on John 4

If the nature of the flesh is considered by itself, it is evidently not life-giving. No created thing has the power to vivify; on the contrary, it itself has need of a life-giving principle. But if we study carefully the mystery of the incarnation, we shall see who it is that inhabits this flesh. Then, if we are not to blaspheme the Holy Spirit, we shall believe that the flesh can give life, despite the fact that of itself the flesh profited nothing. Once it is united to the life-giving Word, it has become wholly life-giving, since it is raised to the power of the Word. The flesh does not bring the Word down to its own level; for the divinity can in no wise be diminished. Of itself the flesh is incapable of imparting life; it can do so only because it has within itself the life-giving Word and because it exercises all the power of the Word. It is the body of life itself, not that of an ordinary man. (Mersch 340)

Commentary: Cyril here explains the power of the miracles of Christ as due to a vital contact with the Word through the medium of his flesh. The condition of such power being shared by the flesh is that it be "his very own flesh, and not that of someone else." It would be someone else's flesh, Cyril is convinced, in the Nestorian view of the incarnation. The same thought is more theoretically expressed in the following passage.

Commentary on John 11.12

Christ comes into us corporally as man, "mingling" and uniting himself with us through the mystery of the "eulogy" [eucharist]; but as God he comes spiritually, by the power and charity of his Spirit, who comes into us to infuse a new life in us and to make us partakers of his divine nature. Thus we see that the bond of our union with God the Father is Christ; as man he unites us with himself, and as God he unites us to God, for he remains truly in the Father. Our nature, subject as it is to corruption, could not attain to incorruption unless the nature that is superior to all corruption and change had come down to us, raised our fallen nature to its own perfection, detached us from the condition of created things through communion and a "mingling" with itself, and transformed into its own likeness us, who are not such by nature. We are perfected in unity with God the Father through our mediator Jesus Christ. For when we receive within us, corporally and spiritually, the true Son who is substantially united with the Father, as I was just saying, we have the glory of participating and communicating in the divine nature. (Mersch 348)

Commentary: It is the flesh of Christ as present in the eucharist which is seen to be the instrument of our divinization. The conception of mediation here is ontological or organic rather than juridical.

Second Letter to Nestorius

Now the holy and great synod [of Nicaea] said that the only-begotten Son himself, by nature begotten from God, even the Father, true God from true God, light from light, through whom the Father made all things, came down, was incarnate, lived as man, suffered, rose the third day, and ascended into heaven. These words and doctrines it behooves us to follow, recognizing what is meant by the Word who is from God being incarnate and living as man.

Commentary: Since this is the letter (to Nestorius) solemnly approved by the Council of Ephesus in 431 as being in accord with Nicaea, some extensive comments are in order. The basic point established from Nicaea is that Nicaea asserts the incarnation, human life, death, and glorification of no other than the eternal Son of God.

For we do not say that the nature of the Word was changed and became flesh, nor that he was transformed into a complete human being, I mean one of soul and body; but this rather, that the Word, having united to himself in his own hypostasis, in an ineffable and inconceivable manner, flesh animated with a rational soul, became man, and was called son of man; not being united merely as a result of will or good pleasure, nor yet by his assumption of a single [human] person; and that while the natures which were brought together into this genuine unity were different, yet of them both is the one Christ and Son, not as though the difference of the natures was abolished by the union, but rather the Godhead and the manhood, by their ineffable and unspeakable consilience into unity, perfected for us the one Lord and Christ and Son.

Commentary: Cyril here first rejects any Apollinarian or monophysite interpretation of his position. "The Word was made flesh" is not to be understood as a metamorphosis of the Word into a body or into a composite of soul and body. It means rather a hypostatic, i.e., real (as opposed to the Nestorian) union of the Word and a complete humanity, so that the Word *is* truly man, not merely *in* a man. The union by "will or good pleasure" was an Antiochene formula understood by Cyril as not a true or hypostatic union. The Word did not assume a human *prosopon* (person). Rather, though the properties of each nature remained, the union was such that there is only one Lord, one Christ, one Son.

And thus, although he had his existence and was begotten from the Father before the ages, he is spoken of as begotten also after the flesh from a woman; not as though his divine nature received its beginning of existence in the holy virgin, nor yet as though a second generation were necessarily wanting for its own sake after that from the Father . . . But when for our sakes and for our salvation the Word, having united humanity to himself hypostatically, came forth from a woman, he is for this reason said to have been born after the flesh. For it was not an ordinary man who was first born of the holy virgin, and upon whom afterwards the Word descended, but he himself, united to humanity from the womb, who is said to have undergone fleshly birth, as making his own the birth of his own flesh.

Commentary: Here Cyril establishes the basis of the *theotokos* (mother of God). The Word truly makes his own the human birth of Mary's son; he truly undergoes human birth. Not, obviously, in his divinity; but he is nevertheless truly born, because this flesh which is born is *his* flesh.

Thus we say that he both suffered and rose again; not meaning that the Word of God, in his own proper [divine] nature, suffered either stripes or the piercing of the nails or any other wounds at all; for the divinity is impassible because it is also incorporeal. But when that which was made his own body suffered, he himself is said to suffer these things for us: for the impassible was in the suffering body.

Commentary: The same doctrine is here extended to the passion and resurrection. Divinity does not suffer, but he who suffers is God as well as man.

Thus we acknowledge one Christ and Lord; not worshiping a man along with the Word, lest a semblance of division might secretly creep in through the use of the words "along with," but worshiping one and the same [Lord], because the Word's body wherein he shares the Father's throne is not alien to himself; in this case again not meaning that there are two Sons in co-session, but one [Son], by reason of his union with his flesh.

Commentary: Here Cyril rejects the co-adoration formula of Nestorius. There is only one Christ, one Son, hence only one adoration, which is directed to the Word incarnate through his flesh.

This [teaching] the statement of the correct faith everywhere sets forth. This we shall find was the view of the holy fathers. Accordingly, they confidently called the holy virgin *theotokos;* not meaning that the nature of the Word or his Godhead received its beginning from the holy virgin, but that, inasmuch as his rationally animated body to which the Word was hypostatically united was born of her, he is said to have been born after the flesh. (ODF 209-11)

Commentary: Here Cyril and the council explicitly endorse the *theotokos*. Elsewhere he says that the entire controversy was about this celebrated term.

The following anathemas were appended by Cyril to his third letter to Nestorius. In some respects they go beyond what was necessary to meet the crisis, and later, in the *Formula of Union* in 433, Cyril will accept a softer language. The third letter, though read at Ephesus, did not receive there the same solemn approbation as the second letter. Subsequent tradition, however, has endorsed it.

Third Letter to Nestorius

3. If, in reference to the one Christ, anyone makes a division of the hypostases after the union, joining them in a mere association of dignity, or of authority or of power, and not, rather, in a real physical union: let him be anathema.

Commentary: Here we have a good instance of Cyril's equating *hypostasis* (person) and *physis* (nature), the latter here in adjectival form and translated as "real, physical." Cyril unwittingly accepted some Apollinarian formulas, thinking they came from Athanasius. The most celebrated of these was "One nature of the Word of God, incarnate." It brought the charge of monophysitism, but it can be shown that he understood it in an orthodox sense, as akin to "One *hypostasis* (person) of the Word of God, incarnate," which he also used. In controversy he was also willing to use a two-nature terminology. A major break-through will be achieved by Chalcedon when it accepts the terminology of one *hypostasis* and one *prosopon* (person), and two natures. Only then does it become terminologically clear that unity and distinction are to be sought on two levels of reality, and what these levels are.

4. If anyone takes the words found in the writings of the gospels and of the apostles, whether they are said of Christ by the saints or of Christ by himself, and distributes them between two persons or hypostases, attributing some of them as to a man, properly understood in contrast to the Word of God, and the rest to the Word of God the Father exclusively, on the grounds that they are proper to God alone: let him be anathema.

Commentary: Though Cyril does not retract this statement in the *Formula of Union,* he does there acknowledge that some of the statements made about Christ in the gospels bring out his unity of person, while others refer to the respective natures. For example, the word "Christ" has been taken by the theologians to signify precisely the union of divinity and humanity, whereas "omnipotence" or "suffering" designate properties of one or other nature.

10. The divine scripture says that Christ became the high priest and apostle of our confession [cf. Heb 3:1], and he offered himself up for us to God the Father in the odor of sweetness [cf. Eph 5:2]. If anyone, therefore, says that it was not the Word of God himself who was born to be our high priest and apostle when he was made flesh [cf. Jn 1:14] and a man like us, but that, properly speaking, it was another

man, distinct from him, who was born of woman; or if anyone says that he presented his offering for himself as well and not solely on our behalf (for as he was sinless, he had no need of any offering): let him be anathema.

Commentary: Here emerge the implications of the controversy for liturgical life. Who is the great high priest? No other than the sinless Word himself, says Cyril, not some man distinct from him.

11. If anyone does not profess that the flesh of the Lord is life-giving and that it belongs to the very Word of God the Father, but professes instead that it belongs to someone other than him, who was linked with him by dignity, or to someone who merely had a divine indwelling; and if he does not profess, rather, that this flesh is life-giving, as we declared, because it was made proper to the Word who has power to give life to all things: let him be anathema. (TCT 168-70)

Commentary: The allusion here is to the eucharistic body of Christ, which is life-giving only because it is the body of none other than the Word himself.

A large number of the Churches of the East, led by John of Antioch, refused to accept the action of Ephesus and in turn anathematized Cyril. In the subsequent mutual efforts at reconciliation, a Christological profession was sent (433) from John to Cyril which the latter accepted. This became known as the *Formula of Union,* and for the moment, at least, peace was restored. The *Formula* is one of the major sources on which the Council of Chalcedon will draw for its definition.

Letter to John of Antioch

We confess, then, our Lord Jesus Christ, only-begotten Son of God, perfect God and perfect man of a rational soul and body, born of the Father before all ages in his Godhead, in the last days the selfsame for us and our salvation born of Mary the virgin in his manhood, consubstantial with the Father in his Godhead, consubstantial with us in his manhood. A union has taken place of two natures. And so we confess one Christ, one Son, one Lord.

Commentary: Worthy of note here are: 1. the emphasis on the fact that it is "the selfsame" who is both God and man; 2. the two-nature formula; 3. the application in Christology of the celebrated *homoousios* (consubstantial). Nicaea had used the term to indicate that the Son was equally divine as the Father, and in the later fourth century it was taken explicitly to convey the numerical identity of substance of Son and Father. Now the *Formula of Union* (followed by Chalcedon) extends the term to convey also the relationship of Christ and other men: he is in his humanity of the same (specific, not numerical, of course) substance or nature as other men, and he is of the very race of men.

According to this same understanding of a union without mixture we confess the holy virgin to be mother of God [*theotokos*] because God the Word was made flesh and became man and from the first moment of conception united to himself the temple he had taken from her. Some of what the apostles and evangelists said about the Lord we know the theologians have attributed to the one person [*prosopon*]. Other sayings they have distinguished as belonging respectively to the two natures [*physeis*], reserving those that befit God to Christ in his divinity while assigning those that are lowly to Christ in his humanity. (ACO 1.1.4. 17)

Commentary: See the remarks made regarding Cyril's fourth anathema, above.

5. EUTYCHES

Introduction

The aged head of a monastery of 300 monks in Constantinople, Eutyches had a reputation for holiness which gave him great influence in court circles. As a theologian, however, he was somewhat confused, and his devotion to Cyril led him to an exaggerated view of the unity of Christ. With Dioscorus, Cyril's successor at Alexandria, he became the center of the reaction against the two-nature doctrine agreed on by Cyril and the Antiochenes in the *Formula of Union.* He insisted on holding to one nature in Christ, and denied that Christ was consubstantial with us. He was brought to trial in a synod at Constantinople in November, 448. The following excerpts from that encounter give an idea of his position.

Trial of Eutyches

Flavian. Do you admit [Christ to be] from two natures?

Commentary: Flavian, patriarch of Constantinople, played a major role in the events preceding Chalcedon. In the present synod he made the very important statement, "We acknowledge that Christ is from [*ek*] two natures after the incarnation, in one hypostasis and one person [*prosopon*] confessing one Christ, one Son, one Lord."

This formula of duality of natures [*physeis*] with unity of *hypostasis* and *prosopon* will become definitive in Chalcedon. But in saying "From [*ek*] two natures" after the incarnation, Flavian gave the monophysites a chance to distinguish (cf. Eutyches' statement, below, and the commentary on Chalcedon). The council will be careful to say "in [*en*] two natures."

Eutyches. Since I acknowledge him as my God and my Lord, the Lord of heaven and earth, I have never yet presumed to theorize about his nature; I admit that I have never said that he is consubstantial with us . . . I confess that the holy virgin is consubstantial with us, and that of her our God was incarnate. . .
Florentius. Since the mother is consubstantial with us, then surely the son is also?
E. Please observe that I have not said that the body of God is the body of man, but that the body was human, and the Lord was made flesh of the virgin. If you wish me to add that he who is of the virgin is consubstantial with us, I will do so . . . but I take the word "consubstantial" in such a way as not to deny that he is the Son of God.
Florentius. Do you or do you not admit that our Lord who is of the virgin is consubstantial and from two natures after the incarnation?
E. I admit that our Lord was from two natures before the union, but after the union one nature . . . I have read of the blessed Cyril and the holy fathers and the holy Athanasius, that they speak of two natures before the union, but after the union and incarnation they speak of one nature, not two.

(ACO 2.1.1. 142-4)

Commentary: Eutyches did not really think that both natures existed before the incarnation, though Leo's *Tome to Flavian* understood him to mean this. Nor was he denying that Christ lacked any element required for true and integral humanity. What he insisted was that this humanity did not form a nature distinct from the divine nature of the Word. He felt he was being faithful to Cyril, even though the latter had accepted also the two-nature formula of Antioch and Rome.

6. LEO THE GREAT

Introduction

As archdeacon of Rome under Pope Celestine I, Leo had occasion to come into contact with the Christological disputes of the East in their Nestorian phase. During his own reign as pope (440-461), he entered more prominently into the picture, especially through his famous *Tome to Flavian.* He was not a great original thinker, but he gave the traditional two-nature Latin Christology magnificent rhetorical expression in the *Tome* and in his sermons. He linked Christology with soteriology, both by his Augustinian stress on Christ the mediator and by his attention to the saving power of the miracles and mysteries of the life of Christ; here his thought has affinities with the physico-mystical theology of the Greeks.

An excellent example of homiletic Christology is furnished by the following Christmas sermon of Leo; the relationship of the incarnation with the redemption and with the Christian life is stressed.

First Christmas Sermon

Today, dearly beloved, our savior is born—let us rejoice! Away with all sorrow on this birthday of life, life which destroys the fear of death, and fills us with joy in the promise of eternity. No one is excluded from a share in this gladness; all have common cause for joy: Our Lord, victor over sin and death, finding no one free from guilt, came for the liberation of all. Let the man in grace exult, for he is close to the palm of victory. Let the sinner rejoice, for pardon is being offered him. Let the pagan take heart, for he is being called to life. For, in the fullness of time [Gal 4:4], that time fixed in the inscrutable depths of divine wisdom, the Son of God clothed himself with man's nature to reconcile it with its creator. Thus the devil, author of death, was to be vanquished by the very nature which he had vanquished. In this struggle on our behalf there was present a profound and wondrous justice: the omnipotent Lord did combat with the savage foe, not through his majesty but through our lowliness, and opposed to him the identical form and nature which shared, indeed, in our mortality, but was free of all sin.

Commentary: We meet again the theme of victory over Satan by justice, not by violence.

And so the Word of God, who is God, the Son of God, who was in the beginning with God, through whom all things were made and without whom nothing was made [cf. Jn 1:1-3], in order to liberate man from eternal death, became man. He stooped down to take upon himself, without diminishing his own majesty, our lowliness, in such wise that, remaining what he was and taking to himself what he was not, he united the true form of a slave to that form in which he is equal to God the Father. He joined the two natures with so perfect a bond that the lower was not consumed by its glorification nor the greater diminished by the assumption. The characteristics of each nature, therefore, are preserved, and unite in a single person: majesty takes on lowliness; power, weakness; eternity, mortality. To pay the debt of our human condition the inviolable nature was united to a suffering one. True God and true man are joined in the unity of the Lord, so that, as our appropriate remedy, one and the same mediator of God and man [1 Tim 2:5] might on the one hand die and on the other rise again . . .

Commentary: These few sentences, in somewhat modified form, will recur in the *Tome to Flavian.*

It was such a birth, dearly beloved, which suited Christ, the power of God and the wisdom of God [cf. 1 Cor 1:24], for thus might he be like us in humanity, above us in divinity. Were he not true God, he could not be a remedy; were he not true man, he could not be a model . . .

Commentary: Here we find again the patristic argument for the need of a God-man as savior.

And so, dearly beloved, let us give thanks to God the Father through his Son in the Holy Spirit. In the great mercy of his love for us he has taken pity on us, and when we were dead in sin he has brought us to life along with Christ [cf. Eph 2:5], that we might be in him a new creation, a new work of his fashioning. And so away with the old man and his deeds! Having attained a share in the birth of Christ, let us renounce the works of the flesh. O Christian, realize your nobility! Now that you have been given a share in the divine nature [cf. 2 Pet 1:4], do not ignobly return to your old meanness. Remember of what head and of what body you are a member! Keep in mind that you have been snatched from the power of darkness and brought into the light of the kingdom of God [Col 1:13]. Through the sacrament of baptism you have been made a temple of the Holy Spirit. Put not to flight by wicked actions so distinguished a guest, nor subject yourself once again to the slavery of the devil. For your ransom is the blood of Christ, and he who redeemed you by his mercy will judge you by his truth, he who with the Father and the Holy Spirit rules for all ages. Amen. (Sermon 21: SC 22.68-74)

Commentary: Leo admirably shows his hearers the dignity that is theirs because of the new creation inaugurated by Christ, head of the mystical body.

Tome to Flavian

In [the] preservation [in Christ] of the real quality of both natures, both being united in one person, lowliness was taken on by majesty, weakness by strength, mortality by the immortal. And in order to pay the debt of our fallen state, inviolable nature was united to one capable of suffering so that (and this is the sort of reparation we needed) one and the same mediator between God and men, the man Jesus Christ [cf. 1 Tim 2:5], could die in the one nature and not die in the other. In the whole and perfect nature of the true man, then, the true

God was born, complete in his own nature, complete in ours . . . He who keeping the form of God created man, the same was made man in an aspect of servitude [cf. Phil 2:7]. Both his natures keep their intrinsic quality without defect; and, just as the aspect of God does not remove the aspect of servitude, so also this latter does not lessen the aspect of God . . .

Commentary: Leo's *Tome to Flavian,* a long letter sent to the patriarch of Constantinople in June, 449, to support him in his struggle with Eutyches and the monophysites, has been called "the most important Christological document of its kind which the Latin Church produced" (Grillmeier 460). In striking rhetoric Leo insists on the perseverance in each nature of its proper characteristics, even though the natures join to form a single person.

The Son of God, then, enters into this weakness of the world, coming down from his heavenly throne, begotten in a new type of birth, but not departing from his Father's glory in the new order . . . He who is true God is also true man; there is no falsity in this union, wherein the lowliness of man and the greatness of the divinity are mutually united. Just as God is not changed by his show of mercy, so the man is not changed by being swallowed up in majesty. Each aspect performs its own acts in cooperation with the other; that is, the Word doing what is proper to the Word, the flesh pursuing what pertains to the flesh. The first of these is ablaze with the miraculous, the other is overpowered by injuries. And just as the Word does not give up any of his equality in the Father's glory, so also the flesh does not abandon the nature of our species. He is one and the same, truly Son of God and truly son of man. (Letter 28: FC 34.95-8)

Commentary: The sentence "Each aspect (*forma*) . . . " provoked some opposition at Chalcedon, because it appeared to make the Word and his flesh two distinct acting subjects or persons. It is balanced, however, by "one and the same." Later, in the monothelite controversy, the former sentence was to be frequently quoted in support of two distinct wills and operations in Christ.

7. THE COUNCIL OF CHALCEDON

Introduction

With the definition of Chalcedon (October, 451), the Church's dogmatic formulation of the mystery of Christ achieves a peak which has never been transcended. The insights of Alexandria, Antioch and Rome were incorporated into a magnificent utterance of the Church's faith in Christ.

The Definition of Chalcedon

Following then the holy fathers,
we all with one voice teach that it should be confessed
that our Lord Jesus Christ is one and the same Son,
the same perfect in Godhead, the same perfect in manhood,
truly God and truly man,
the same [consisting of] a rational soul and a body;
homoousios [consubstantial] with the Father as to his Godhead,
and the same *homoousios* with us as to his manhood;
in all things like unto us, sin only excepted;
begotten of the Father before ages as to his Godhead,
and in the last days, the same,
for us and for our salvation,
of Mary the virgin, *theotokos* [mother of God] as to his manhood;
one and the same Christ, Son, Lord, only-begotten,
made known in two natures [which exist]
without confusion, without change, without division, without separation;
the difference of the natures having been in no wise taken away by reason of the union,
but rather the properties of each nature being preserved,
and both concurring into one person [*prosopon*] and one hypostasis —
not parted or divided into two persons [*prosopa*],
but one and the same Son and only-begotten, the divine *Logos,* the Lord Jesus Christ:
even as the prophets from of old have spoken concerning him,

and as the Lord Jesus Christ himself has taught us,
and as the symbol of the fathers has delivered to us.

(Sellers 210-11).

Commentary: Following . . . Fathers. The bishops at Chalcedon were reluctant to formulate a new creed, and when forced to it prefaced their definition by repeating the creeds of Nicaea (325) and Constantinople I (381).

One and the same. This traditional expression (cf. Irenaeus) occurs three times in the definition, and the shorter "the same" occurs five times. Hence it would be wrong to see in Chalcedon a mere Antiochene reaction against Cyril. What is especially admirable is the simultaneous affirmation of unity and distinction.

Perfect in Godhead . . . in manhood. Note the several antitheses in the first part of the definition, bringing out duality.

Homoousios (consubstantial). On this double consubstantiality, which marvellously unites trinitarian and Christological faith, see the commentary on the *Formula of Union.* Eutyches' initial refusal to accept the consubstantiality of Christ with us is here envisaged.

In two natures. Not merely "from two natures." This last formula was used in an early draft of the definition, but it was quickly seen that it left room for the monophysite distinction: "from two natures before the union, but one nature after the union."

Without confusion . . . separation. Here are the famous four adverbs, the first two excluding monophysitism, the second excluding Nestorianism. "Without separation" also excludes, it would seem from the historical context, the separation of the Word from his body between death and resurrection.

The difference . . . union. This passage is from Cyril's second letter to Nestorius, and shows that the monophysites were wrong to appeal to him for support.

The properties . . . one person. This is an echo of Leo's *Tome* and indirectly also of Tertullian; yet it is in accord with Cyril's second letter to Nestorius.

And one hypostasis. We have seen Flavian's use of "one hypostasis and one person." Terminologically, this is probably the crucial point: where Cyril had tended to make *physis* and *hypostasis* equivalents, Chalcedon separated them, and gave them the role of expressing, respectively, duality and unity, or, we may say, the "what" (divinity and humanity) and the "who" (the person of the Word) of the God-man.

Even as . . . to us. The bishops of Chalcedon conceived that they were not innovating, but echoing in a new form scripture and previous tradition. "The dogma of Chalcedon is ancient tradition in a formula corresponding to the needs of the hour" (Grillmeier 487).

QUESTIONS FOR DISCUSSION

1. What aspect of Christ's ontic constitution does Athanasius neglect? Who makes up for this lack?
2. Illustrate Apollinarius' use of the soteriological argument. What was he trying to prove?
3. What did Apollinarius deny in his Christology?
4. What did Gregory of Nazianzus defend in his first letter to Cledonius? Why is this important?
5. How did Gregory of Nyssa express the physico-mystical conception of redemption?
6. What is meant by the term *assumptus homo?*
7. What patristic writer united in his doctrine both western and eastern traditions?
8. What does Jerome emphasize in his writings?
9. What was the context within which Ambrose's Christological teaching was formulated?
10. Indicate some important Augustinian themes.
11. Why did Diodore of Tarsus object to Apollinarianism? Illustrate.
12. Describe Theodore of Mopsuestia's predominant view of the redemption.
13 What was the difficulty Nestorius had with the term *theotokos?*
14. What contribution did Cyril of Alexandria make toward clarifying the term *theotokos?*
15. What position did Eutyches actually maintain with regard to Christ's humanity?
16. What is the importance of Pope Leo's *Tome to Flavian?* Explain.
17. How did Cyril's understanding of *physis* and *hypostasis* differ from that of Chalcedon? Did Chalcedon's formulation have any unfortunate results?

CHAPTER 3

AFTER CHALCEDON

Prefatory Note

Though Chalcedon represented a breakthrough in Christological understanding, it resulted in the serious schism of the monophysite churches of Syria and Egypt. Christological development and controversy for the next two centuries and more will center about two vain efforts to reconcile the dissidents.

The first of these efforts culminates a century after Chalcedon in the Second Council of Constantinople. Dominated by Emperor Justinian, it is a victory for the Alexandrian spirit in Christology. From the West of this period, we have selected two notable documents, the influential *Quicumque* creed, with its advanced Christological formulations, and the speculations on person and nature of Boethius, which were to have a great influence in the Middle Ages.

In the seventh century, the Mohammedan threat stimulated a further effort to reconcile the monophysites. Now the Christological issue moves from the sphere of person and nature to that of wills and activities. Pope Honorius imprudently encourages the one-will theory (monothelitism), but is repudiated along with the theory by the Third Council of Constantinople in 681, which, in emphasis, is a victory for the Antiochene spirit. We may, with some oversimplification, say that the four Christological councils from Ephesus in 431 to Third Constantinople in 681 alternated between the Alexandrian and the Antiochene emphasis.

From the earlier seventh century we have chosen a passage from Gregory the Great on the knowledge of Christ; and to conclude the entire patristic period some texts from John Damascene, who summed up the enduring Christological doctrine of his predecessors, and who was to be an important medium for the influence of eastern Christology on St. Thomas and subsequent theology in the West to our own day.

A. From Chalcedon to the Second Council of Constantinople

1. THE QUICUMQUE CREED

Introduction

The creed which begins *"Quicumque"* ("Whoever . . . ") was long attributed to St. Athanasius and went by the name of the Athanasian creed. It is certainly not his work. Most probably it is of western origin, dating from the fifth or sixth centuries; southern Gaul is where it most likely came from. Its author remains unknown. The first part is trinitarian, the second part, given here in full, is Christological. It is an admirable dogmatic summary of the two basic mysteries of Christianity, and at an early date it won in the West a standing comparable to the Apostles' and Nicene creeds, and a place in the liturgy.

It is also necessary for eternal salvation that he [whoever wishes to be saved] believe steadfastly in the incarnation of our Lord Jesus Christ. The true faith is: we believe and profess that our Lord Jesus Christ, the Son of God, is both God and man. As God he was begotten of the substance of the Father before time; as man he was born in time of the substance of his mother. He is perfect God; and he is perfect man, with a rational soul and human flesh. He is equal to the Father in his divinity but he is inferior to the Father in his humanity. Although he is God and man, he is not two but one Christ. And he is one, not because his divinity was changed into flesh, but because his humanity was assumed to God. He is one, not at all because of a mingling of substances, but because he is one person.

Commentary: Compare this Christological formula (two substances, one person) with the trinitarian formula in the first part of the *Quicumque,* "without mingling the persons or dividing the substance," and with the liturgy's preface of the Trinity, "not with the oneness of a single person, but with the trinity of a single substance."

As a rational soul and flesh are one man, so God and man are one Christ.

Commentary: Here the comparison between the incarnation and the soul-body structure of man achieves its highest dogmatic expression. The comparison not only gives us the best understanding of the mystery of Christ (so far as understanding is possible) but brings together in a single statement the mystery of Christ and the mystery of man.

He died for our salvation, descended to hell, arose from the dead on the third day, ascended into heaven, sits at the right hand of God the Father almighty, and from there he shall come to judge the living and the dead. At his coming, all men are to arise with their own bodies; and they are to give an account of their lives. Those who have done good deeds will go into eternal life; those who have done evil will go into everlasting fire. This is the Catholic faith. Everyone must believe it, firmly and steadfastly; otherwise, he cannot be saved.

(TCT 5-6)

2. BOETHIUS

Introduction

Though Boethius (d. 525) is more philosopher than theologian, he made one classic contribution to Christological development: he evolved, by Aristotelian dialectic, notions of nature and person which he applied to the refutation of the two extreme positions. It was especially his definition of person as "an individual substance of a rational nature" which contributed greatly to medieval speculation. Though this notion finally proved inadequate, his method of seeking, in the definitions and differences of nature and person, tools for understanding the mystery of Christ, was a beacon for succeeding ages.

Treatise against Eutyches and Nestorius 1-5

Let me first clear away the extreme and self-contradictory errors of Nestorius and Eutyches; after that, by God's help, I will temperately set forth the middle way of the Christian faith. But since in this whole question of self-contradictory heresies the matter of debate is persons and natures, these terms must first be defined and distinguished by their proper differences.

[After distinguishing several senses of "nature":] Nature has, further, another meaning according to which we speak of the different nature of gold and silver, wishing thereby to point the special property of things; this meaning of nature will be defined as follows: "Nature is the specific difference that gives form to anything." Thus, although nature is described or defined in all these different ways, both Catholics and Nestorians firmly hold that there are in Christ two natures of the kind laid down in our last definition, for the same specific differences cannot apply to God and man.

But the proper definition of person is a matter of very great perplexity. For if every nature has person, the difference between nature and person is a hard knot to unravel; or if person is not taken as the equivalent of nature but is a term of less scope and range, it is difficult to say to what natures it may be extended, that is, to what natures the term person may be applied and what natures are dissociate from it. For one thing is clear, namely that nature is a substrate of person, and that person cannot be predicated apart from nature . . .

Commentary: He then goes on to show that person cannot be affirmed of bodies without life, or of living things without sense, or indeed of whatever is bereft of mind and reason; further, person does not apply to universals, but to individuals. Then:

Wherefore, if person belongs to substances alone, and these rational, and if every nature is a substance, existing not in universals but in individuals, we have found the definition of person—i.e., "an individual substance of a rational nature."

Commentary: The achievement of Boethius' definition is the clear expression of the elements necessary and sufficient for the constitution of the person, and the notes which distinguish it from nature, i.e., rationality and substantiality. Its limitation is that it does not provide for the distinction between the individuality within a species which is characteristic of each nature, including the humanity of Christ, and that individuality (which the scholastics will refer to as "incommunicability") which is characteristic of the person as such, and which is therefore not present in the human nature of Christ. But Boethius' definition is an important step towards this sharper notion of person.

For the time being let that distinction between nature and person hold which I have affirmed—i.e., that nature is the specific property of any substance, and person the individual substance of a rational nature . . . I must now pass to Eutyches who asserts that, so far from our having to believe in a twofold person in Christ, we must not even confess a double nature; humanity, he maintains, was so assumed that the union with Godhead involved the disappearance of the human nature. His error springs from the same source as that of Nestorius. For just as Nestorius judges there could not be a double nature unless the person were doubled, and therefore, confessing the double nature in Christ, has perforce believed the person to be double, so also Eutyches judged that the nature was not double unless the person was double, and since he did not confess a double person, he thought it a necessary consequence that the nature should be regarded as single. Thus Nestorius, rightly holding Christ's nature to be double, sacrilegiously professes the persons to be two; whereas Eutyches, rightly believing the person to be single, impiously believes that the nature also is single. And being confuted by the plain evidence of facts, since it is clear that the nature of God is different from that of man, he declares his belief to be: two natures in Christ before the union and only one after the union.

(LCL 77-101)

Commentary: Being a logician and not a historian, Boethius presents a somewhat gross and abstract idea of the two heretical positions. However, he does have the keenness to see that, after Chalcedon's clear assertion of two natures and one person, the theological problem is concerned with the conceptual distinction of nature and person. In the East after Chalcedon, a similar speculative development was taking place, in Leontius of Byzantium and others.

3. THE SECOND COUNCIL OF CONSTANTINOPLE

Introduction

The Second Council of Constantinople in 553 was very much Emperor Justinian's council. Anxious for reconciliation with the monophysites, who had rejected Chalcedon's two-nature teaching, he pressed Pope Vigilius to join in a condemnation of the "Three Chapters," i.e., certain works of three Antiochene theologians of the era of Ephesus and Chalcedon: Theodore of Mopsuestia, Theodoret of Cyr, and Ibas of Edessa. The pope, after much reluctance and suffering, finally approved the council's anathemas, whose strongly anti-Antiochene character is explained by Justinian's intent. The council never won enthusiastic support in the West. Justinian's ecumenical effort was in vain, for the monophysites continued in schism.

Anathematisms of the Three Chapters

8. If anyone, though professing that the union was made from two natures, from divinity and humanity, or though saying that there is one incarnate nature of the Word of God, does not understand these expressions in the same sense as the holy fathers taught, namely, that the hypostatic union of the divine and the human natures resulted in one Christ; but if, instead, he tries in consequence of such expressions to introduce a single nature, or substance, of Christ's divinity and humanity: let such a one be anathema.

Commentary: Here the council gives the orthodox understanding of Cyril's controversial phrase, "one incarnate nature of the Word of God," which the monophysites had insisted on following, and because of which they saw Nestorianism in the two-nature terminology of Chalcedon.

9. If anyone says that Christ is adored in two natures, and thus introduces two adorations, one proper to the divine Word, the other proper to the man; or if, in order to destroy the humanity or to commingle the divinity and the humanity, anyone speaks falsely of a single nature or substance of the natures that have come together, and in this sense adores Christ; but does not rather adore with a single adoration the divine Word incarnate with his own flesh, according to the tradition in the Church of God from the beginning: let such a one be anathema.

Commentary: What is being rejected here is not the adoration of Christ in two natures, but a double adoration or co-adoration in the sense of Nestorius, together with any single adoration based on the monophysite conception of Christ's unity.

10. If anyone does not profess that our Lord Jesus Christ who was crucified in his humanity is truly God and Lord of glory and one of the holy trinity: let such a one be anathema.

Commentary: This anathema reflects the controversial slogan of the period, "One of the Trinity has suffered (or: been crucified)." The statement is a legitimate application of the principle of mutual predication of properties. But it was also used by the monophysites and so came under suspicion. Here it is accepted, undoubtedly in an effort to please the monophysites.

12. If anyone defends the irreverent Theodore of Mopsuestia who said that God the Word is one person, while Christ is another person who was subject to disturbance by the passions of the soul and by the desires of the body, but who was gradually set free from inferior inclinations; and thus being made better through the improvement of his works, and becoming irreproachable by his conduct, he was baptized, though a mere man, in the name of the Father and Son and Holy Spirit; and through the baptism received the grace of the

Holy Spirit, and was deemed worthy of adoption; and, as in the case of an imperial image, he is worshiped out of respect for the person of God the Word; and after his resurrection he has become steadfast in purpose and wholly incapable of sin. Furthermore, the same irreverent Theodore has said that the union of God the Word with Christ is the same kind as the apostle describes in the case of man and wife: "The two shall become one flesh". . . (Eph 5:31). Let such a one be anathema. (DS 429-34; TCT 423-7)

Commentary: Here the council is refusing any theory of moral growth in Christ that would make him at any time subject to concupiscence in the pejorative sense, and would postpone his utter sinlessness till after the resurrection.

B. Third Constantinople and the Close of the Patristic Era

1. GREGORY THE GREAT

Introduction

This pope (d. 604) was no major personal contributor to progress in Christology. He was primarily a preacher and administrator. But his position and influence made him an important link between the patristic (especially Augustinian) and medieval worlds. The single passage given here indicates one important area of Christology where he represents such a link.

Letter to Eulogius

Concerning that passage, "Of that day and hour neither the Son knows nor the angels" [Mk 13:32], your holiness is entirely correct in judging that it is not to be referred to that same Son insofar as he is head but to his body which we are . . . [Augustine] also says that it can be referred to the Son because almighty God sometimes speaks in human fashion. Just as we call a day joyful not because the day itself is but because it makes us joyful, so the almighty Son says he does not know the day which he causes to be not known, not because he himself does not know but because he does not permit it to be known. So the Father alone is said to know because the Son who is consubstantial with him knows from his [divine] nature what the angels do not know. Thus it can be understood that the incarnate Son, become perfect man for us, knows the day and the hour *in* his human nature but it is not *from* his human nature that he knows it. What he knows in his humanity he does not know from it because the God-man knows the day and the hour by the power of his divinity . . . God and man knows the day and the hour. But he knows it because God is man. It is absolutely clear, then, that whoever is not a Nestorian cannot be an agnoete. For if he professes that the very wisdom of God is incarnate, how can he intelligently state that there is anything which the wisdom of God does not know? (DS 474-6)

Commentary: The agnoetes (Gk *agnoeo* — to be ignorant of) were a sixth-century monophysite sect under Themistius who, on the basis of Mk 13:32 and other passages, attributed ignorance to the human mind of Christ. Gregory took part in the ensuing dispute in this letter to Eulogius, the patriarch of Constantinople, in 600. We see here an expression of the growing anti-Nestorian tendency of the later patristic era: to deny that the human mind of the savior could be in any way ignorant.

2. POPE HONORIUS

Introduction

This pope (d. 638) is celebrated for allowing himself to be drawn into a semi-endorsement of the position of the monothelites, i.e., those who maintained that in Christ there was only one will and one operation *(energeia)*. Honorius, it would seem, was badly informed on the issues then agitating the East. He wrote two unfortunate letters (634) to Sergius, patriarch of Constantinople, one of the leaders of those who sought to win back the monophysites by certain doctrinal concessions having to do with the voluntary activity of the God-man. The letters won support in the East for the monothelites, but also opposition to Honorius in both East and West. A successor, John IV, pointed out in defense of Honorius that in excluding two wills he was quite rightly excluding a moral contrariety of wills. But Honorius was anathematized along with Sergius and others by the Third Council of Constantinople (681), and the condemnation was confirmed by Pope Leo II in 682.

First Letter to Sergius

We confess that there was one will of our Lord Jesus Christ, because certainly it was our nature, not our fault, which was assumed by the divinity, that nature which was made before sin, not the one vitiated by the fall . . . The savior did not possess another law in his members [cf. Rom 7:23] nor a divided or contrary will since he was born above the law of the human condition.

Commentary: It seems clear from the context that Honorius is only excluding here all moral conflict between the human and divine wills in Christ. Yet this was not an issue between the disputing parties, and Honorius' failure to condemn the doctrine which denied a human will in Christ was an unfortunate victory for the monothelites.

The sacred scriptures are filled with clear indications that our Lord Jesus Christ is the one agent [*operator*] in both his divinity and humanity. Whether, on account of the actions of his divinity and humanity, one should speak about and understand a single or a double activity is not a matter worth our concern. We leave such subtle disputes for the grammarians to peddle to schoolboys. The scriptures do not tell us about one or two activities of our Lord Jesus Christ and his Holy Spirit. Rather they speak of his manifold activity . . . The mediator of God and men acts fully and perfectly and in manifold and ineffable ways in the communion of both natures . . . We repudiate this new terminology which is breeding scandal in the holy churches of God. We do not want the little ones [cf. Mt 18:6] to be scandalized by the phrase "two activities" and to think that we have followed the Nestorians in their madness. Nor, on the other hand, do we wish, by speaking of one activity of our Lord Jesus Christ, to seem to be professing the foolish insanity of the Eutychians . . .

(PL 80.472-4; cf. DS 487)

Commentary: Honorius desires to speak neither of one nor of two operations, but is content to say that Christ acted perfectly and in manifold ways in the communion of both natures. The sixth ecumenical council will make the choice which Honorius refused.

3. THE THIRD COUNCIL OF CONSTANTINOPLE

Introduction

The sixth ecumenical council at Constantinople in 681 brought the long controversy on the human will and activities of Christ to its resolution. The monothelite position was excluded, and duality of will and activity was defined. Despite Honorius' unfortunate compromise decades earlier, Pope Martin I in a Lateran synod (649) and especially Pope Agatho in two letters to the emperors (680) prepared the way for the council's definition. Repeating the definition of Chalcedon, the council extended the Christological one-and-many to the sphere of Christ's volition and activity. Negatively, it anathematized the monothelites and Honorius.

Council Teaching

And we furthermore teach that in him were two natural volitions or wills and two natural activities, undivided, unchanged, inseparable, unmixed, according to the teachings of the holy fathers; and that the two natural wills were not opposed to one another, as the impious heretics assert, God forbid, but that his human will followed without resistance or reluctance, subject to his divine and omnipotent will.

Commentary: 1. "Natural" is used here of the wills and activities of Christ in the sense of "pertaining to the natures"; it is not, of course, denied that it is the person or hypostasis which acts in and through each nature; 2. the four adverbs of Chalcedon (in different sequence) are now extended to the wills and activities of Christ; 3. the objection of the monothelites is forestalled by pointing out that there is no question of moral opposition between the human and divine wills.

It was necessary that his fleshly will move itself, but at the same time be subjected to the divine will [others translate: it was necessary that his fleshly will be moved (i.e., put into action), and even subjected to the divine will], as the all-wise Athanasius declared [in a lost treatise].

Commentary: The alternative translation, in brackets, stresses exclusively the limitations of the human will; the other translation has the council affirming the spontaneous and active character of the human will, along with the necessity of its moral conformity to the divine will.

For just as his flesh is called and is the flesh of God the Word, so the natural will of his flesh is called and is the property of God the Word. Just as his most holy, innocent, and animated flesh, though divinized, was not taken away but remained in its own proper state and condition, so too, his human will, though divinized, is not destroyed, but rather is all the more preserved.

Commentary: The council argues to the necessity of the sinlessness of Christ's human will from the fact that it has been, like his flesh, made the property of the Word. Yet this moral identity of wills does not destroy physical distinction.

We likewise glorify the two natural activities, undivided, unchanged, unmixed, inseparable, in the same Lord of ours, Jesus Christ, our true God, that is to say: a divine activity and a human activity, according to Leo, teacher of things divine, who clearly asserts: "Each form does its own proper work in communion with the other, the Word working what belongs to the Word and the flesh what belongs to the flesh" [cf. above, *Tome of Leo*].

Commentary: From the question of volition the council moves on to speak of activity (*energeia*). The famous sentence from the *Tome of Leo* is invoked.

We do not in any sense admit that there is but one natural activity of God and the creature, so as not to elevate the creature to the level of divine being, nor degrade the uniqueness of the divine nature to the level proper to the created.

(Mansi 11.635-7; DS 556-7)

4. JOHN DAMASCENE

Introduction

The man usually treated as the last of the Greek fathers, John of Damascus (d. 749) offers in book 3 of his *Orthodox Faith* a splendid Christological synthesis, drawn from his predecessors. Damascene is inclined to extend to a maximum the human wisdom of Christ, but on the other hand he stresses the necessity of a true human will in the savior for the healing of our fallen wills.

Holy Images 16

I honor all matter and venerate it. Through it, filled, as it were, with a divine power and grace, my salvation has come to me. Was not the thrice happy and thrice blessed wood of the cross matter? Was not the sacred and holy mountain of Calvary matter? What of the life-giving rock, the holy sepulchre, the source of our resurrection: was it not matter? Is not the most holy book of the gospels matter? Is not the blessed table matter which gives us the bread of life? Are not the gold and silver matter, out of which crosses and altarplate and chalices are made? And before all these things, is not the body and blood of our Lord matter? Either do away with the veneration and worship due to all these things, or submit to the tradition of the Church in the worship of images, honoring God and his friends, and following in this the grace of the Holy Spirit. Do not despise matter, for it is not despicable. (Allies 16-17)

Commentary: The incarnation affects the Christian's view of all things. The eighth-century iconoclast dispute (settled by the Second Council of Nicaea in 787) was a consequence of the earlier Christological controversies.

The Orthodox Faith 3.3

Moreover, the Word makes human things his own, because what is proper to his sacred flesh belongs to him; and the things which are his own he communicates to his flesh. This is after the manner of exchange [*antidosis*] on account of the mutual immanence [*perichoresis*] of the parts and the hypostatic union and because he who, "with each form cooperating with the other, performed" both divine and human acts was one and the same (see *Tome of Leo* above). Wherefore the Lord of glory is even said to have been crucified [cf. 1 Cor 2:8], although his divine nature did not suffer; and the son of man is confessed to have been in heaven before his passion, as the Lord himself has said [cf. Jn 3:13]. (FC 37.274)

Commentary: Perichoresis or circumincession (mutual immanence) expresses both trinitarian and Christological relationships of distinction within unity. This is the objective basis for the exchange *(antidosis),* i.e., mutual predication of properties.

The Orthodox Faith 3.7

One must know, moreover, that, although we say that the natures of the Lord are mutually immanent [*perichorein*], we know that this immanence comes from the divine nature. For this last pervades all things and indwells as it wishes, but nothing pervades it. And it communicates its splendors to the body while remaining impassible and having no part in the affections of the body. (FC 37.284)

Commentary: The mutual immanence of humanity and divinity is unequal. The Word does not receive but only communicates in the relationship.

The Orthodox Faith 3.9

Now, although there is no nature *without* subsistence [*anhypostatos*] or substance without person, because both the substance and the nature are only to be found in subsistences and persons, it is unnecessary for natures hypostatically united to each other to be provided each with its own subsistence . . . The flesh of the Word of God was not independently subsistent nor was there any other person besides that of the Word of God. On the contrary, it was *in* the person of the Word that the flesh subsisted, or, rather, had personality [*enhypostatos*], and it did not become an independently subsisting person in itself. For this reason, it neither lacks personality nor introduces another person into the Trinity. (FC 37.286-7)

Commentary: From Leontius of Byzantium Damascene derives the distinction between an "impersonal" (*anhypostatos*) nature and a nature personalized not in itself but in the person of another nature. The latter is the case with Christ. By the fact that the humanity is *in* the Word, it subsists by the divine personality.

The Orthodox Faith 3.22

He is said to have progressed in wisdom and age and grace [cf. Lk 2:52], because he did increase in age and by this increase in age brought more into evidence the wisdom inherent in him; further, because by making what is ours altogether his own he made his own the progress of men in wisdom and grace . . . Now, those who say that he progressed in wisdom and grace in the sense of receiving an increase in these are saying that the union was not made from the first instant of the flesh's existence. Neither are they holding the hypostatic union, but, misled by the empty-headed Nestorius, they are talking preposterously of a relative union and simple indwelling . . . For, if from the first instant of its existence the flesh was truly united to God the Word—rather, had existence in him and identity of person with him—how did it not enjoy perfectly all wisdom and grace? (FC 37.326-7)

Commentary: This is an instance of the growing tendency to deny limits to the human knowledge of Christ.

Two Wills 28

If he did not assume a human will, he did not heal that in us which was the first to be wounded. Now, as Gregory the theologian [Nazianzen; see his letter to Cledonius above] said, "What has not been assumed has not been healed." But what had stumbled if not the will? And so it was that which had stumbled, that which had sinned, which was more in need of the remedy. But if you say that he did not assume the will which had sinned, then neither did he assume the nature which had sinned. If he did not assume this, then he did not assume human nature, for it is human nature which had sinned. (PG 95.161)

Commentary: The soteriological argument is here applied to show the need of a human will in Christ.

Two Wills 42

Just as, through his bodily activity, his divine will was at work . . . so through his human will his divine will was at work. For by divinely willing he worked the miracle [cf. Lk 7:14] and by humanly willing he stretched forth his hand and said, "Arise." And so, in brief, whatever he willed and did humanly was the salvation of the world. For he did not accomplish divine things in a purely divine way, nor did he perform human things in a purely human way. For it was not the sufferings of a mere man which saved the world. Rather, being God and becoming man, he displayed a certain new and wondrous and theandric activity: divine, but working through the human; human, but ministering to the divine, and manifesting in sign the divinity conjoined with it. (PG 95.181-4)

Commentary: John Damascene here takes from the pseudo-Dionysian corpus (c.500) the notion of "theandric operation," that is, activity at once divine and human. It was at one time suspect because of the use made of it by the monothelites, but was subsequently accepted in Catholic circles. Where the definition of 681 is Antiochene in emphasis, this term is Alexandrian.

QUESTIONS FOR DISCUSSION

1. In the seventh century, Christological discussion shifted away from its concentration on person and nature. What was the new focus?
2. "As a rational soul and flesh are one man, so God and man are one Christ." From what document is this quotation taken, and what is its significance?

3. What was Boethius' contribution to Christological development and why is it important? Indicate the good and bad features of Boethius' definition.
4. Did the Second Council of Constantinople (553) accept the idea of moral growth in Christ? Explain.
5. Who were the agnoetes?
6. Why is Pope Honorius an ecclesiastical celebrity? Explain the monothelite dispute and Honorius' part in it.
7. What did the Third Council of Constantinople (681) clarify with regard to Christ's human will?
8. John of Damascene tended to deny limits to the human knowledge of Christ. How does this relate to the notion of "theandric operation"?

CONCLUSION

Why should one idle spade, I wonder,
Shake up the dust of thanes like thunder
To smoke and choke the sun?
In clouds of clay, so cast to heaven,
What shape shall man discern?
G. K. Chesterton, *The Ballad of the White Horse.*

Many minds today tend to be impatient or diffident when they encounter studies of the distant past which make no explicit reference to current concerns. Other times, other men, other problems: except for the privileged case of the inspired writings, irrelevance is often the unspoken epithet with which the theology of other days is dismissed. And there is no small portion of truth contained in such an attitude. To be true to itself, patristic theology in its study of the past must stand in the present and be concerned for the future. True, it must be willing to leave its own age and enter into the past, in the sense that it must put aside anachronism and eisegesis and seek, so far as possible, to look at Christ and the world with the eyes of Origen and Cyril and Augustine. But to deserve a hearing today, it must be willing to show what the fathers have to say to the Christian of today.

It is with this question that we conclude our brief anthology of patristic Christology. Apart from any insights or inspiration received from this or that particular text, what profit may we gain from the reflections of the Church fathers on the person and work of Jesus Christ? For convenience we may speak first of the *form,* then of the *content,* of the Christological dogma as it emerged in the first several centuries.

By *form* here we mean the fathers' characteristic mode of

theologizing on the mystery of the incarnation, their intellectual habits and attitudes. We would suggest that, from this point of view, patristic Christology offers *five values* of great importance for today:

First, a sense of development. By this we mean an acknowledgement of the legitimacy and necessity of going beyond the categories in which the original revelation was made, in order to seek, within the identical faith of the apostolic age, a clearer understanding of faith. It has been well said that Arianism, and perhaps other heresies as well, was a kind of unadventurous archaism and primitivism, unwilling to let go of traditional formulations or to assume new ones, and by that very fact betraying traditional doctrine. Doctrinal development represents the adventure of orthodoxy, as Chesterton set forth so eloquently; it is heterodoxy which, at least by hindsight, is seen to be a plodding repetition of phrases once vital but now dead because arrested in their potential for growth.

A sense of legitimate and necessary development, then, in language and in concept, is characteristic of patristic Christology in its unfolding toward Ephesus and Chalcedon and beyond. Greek philosophy was the catalyst of this change. The movement was from the functional, dynamic categories of the inspired (and for the most part Semitic) authors, to the ontological categories derived from Platonism, stoicism and other philosophical traditions.

Having said this, we must immediately add that, just as fidelity to the original deposit involved for the fathers a willingness to go beyond the original deposit, so, on our part, fidelity to the fathers and to the dogma of Chalcedon involves willingness to go beyond the fathers and Chalcedon. In Karl Rahner's often quoted phrase, Chalcedon is both end and beginning. There are other modes of Christian reflection on the mystery of Christ than the ones employed by the fathers; there are other philosophical insights than those of Plato and Aristotle which may be enlisted in the cause of theological understanding. Hence, fidelity to Chalcedon today means willingness to finish the work which Chalcedon began. Concretely this means not only a continuation of speculation on the traditional concepts of person and nature, but, more important, a new kind of reflection which will systematically avoid speaking in terms of these concepts of person and nature, and will employ distinctively modern contributions to human thought. Recent insights into cosmic and human evolution, into the human person as conscious and free subject, into human life as intersubjective—these are the catalysts being used today to further the progress of Christology.

In this, our contemporary task, we will be helped by a *second* characteristic of patristic Christology, namely, *constant recourse to scripture* as the privileged and inexhaustible font of Christological wisdom. We have seen enough of patristic Christology to realize that it was the result of an unceasing pondering of the bible. Here many people today may be tempted to dismiss and even scoff at patristic exegesis, which certainly was deficient, sometimes naively so, in the tools and techniques developed during the past century. But it would be a grave mistake to miss the fact that the fathers' doctrinal portrait of Christ, while drawing on philosophical conceptions familiar to their age, represented a deep penetration of the letter of scripture to the underlying spirit and sense. No one has better expressed this value of patristic exegesis for our day than Pierre Benoit. His statement is all the more eloquent in that it comes from one of our best critical exegetes:

> We are not only westerners but moderns, who have gone through the crisis of rationalism and remain imbued with its scientific positivism. In spite of ourselves, rational truth has come to take precedence with us over religious truth. Hence the itch for material accuracy, the mania for the detail of the event, so that we forget its significance as a sign, which alone counts in the end. "We strain out the gnat but swallow the camel" (Mt 23:24). Such critical exigency is useful, but in its subordinate role; it must not be a shortsightedness which prevents us from seeing the horizon. "These things you ought to have done, while not leaving the others undone" (Mt 23:23). The ancient sacred writers, who saw in everything the problem of God, reached better

> than we the essential truth of history, even if they did not keep so close to accuracy of the details. And the fathers of the Church, Greek and Latin as they were, still had that religious sense which made them go straight to the substance, without becoming entangled in minor defects. It is that sense of faith that we must recover if we also wish to hear what the bible wants to say to us. Then many false problems will disappear. We shall find in the bible the full truth, because we shall look for it there solely where God has placed it. (*Guide to the Bible,* vol. 1, ed. A. Robert & A. Tricot. New York, 1960, p. 51)

It was perhaps this connaturality with scripture which endowed the Christology of the fathers with a *third* characteristic, *a feeling for the unity of Christian doctrine*. Vatican I in a famous statement assigns a threefold task to theological understanding of Christian mystery: 1. penetration into each mystery with the help of truths of the natural order; 2. comparison of the mysteries among themselves; 3. the referral of each and all the mysteries to man's salvation. The first of these tasks, which is most characteristic of scholastic theology, was certainly not neglected by the fathers. But it is the second and the third task in which they especially excel. In their stage of Christian development, mysteries are rarely studied in isolation. The synthetic rather than the analytic predominates. Christology, even where it is concerned with the basic structure of the God-man, is never far from soteriology, and both are interwoven with ecclesiology and with the theology of the Trinity, grace and the sacraments. We have found expression of this in our booklet especially in the frequent recurrence of the axiom, "What is not assumed is not healed." This constant preoccupation with the mutual interaction of all the mysteries of the faith, and with their value for our salvation, is a characteristic both congenial to our modern mentality (weary of the atomization to which so much of scholasticism has succumbed) and a salutary reminder of the unity of Christian faith and of theology.

A very similar value is found in a *fourth* characteristic, namely, *the pastoral orientation of patristic Christology*. By and large, the works we have been examining were not scholarly tomes but sermons, letters, polemical and apologetical literature, utterances of the official teachers of the faithful, the bishops of the Church. Never in the life of the Church (except, perhaps, for the era now dawning) has theology been so close to the people and their needs. That theology is a service of the entire people of God, that sound doctrine has repercussions in the moral and religious life of Christians—these too are insights we may derive from the Christology of the fathers.

Fifthly (and finally), there is *a sense of mystery.* The risk of seeking a development of understanding in the mysteries of faith with the help of rational categories is that it will degenerate into a mere philosophy, a spinning out of ideas, a deduction of one abstraction from another. Scholasticism in its worst hours has succumbed to this temptation. The great scholastics have not. Even so, there is in the very genre of scholastic theology something which tends to make the rational the dominant trait, and the mysterious the recessive. This is legitimate. There are times when clarity and precision are so urgently needed by the people of God that the risk of overshadowing the mystery must be taken. Romano Guardini has put it beautifully in his comparison of our two greatest theologians: Christian thought protects itself from depriving the finite of its power "by making Augustine guardian of the inner sanctuary, but Thomas Aquinas its guide" (*The Conversion of Augustine.* Westminster, 1960, p. 103). Patristic theology, by and large, reverses the order of prominence of the rational and the mysterious. Perhaps we may express the difference by saying that the traditional description of theology as *intelligentia fidei* (*understanding* of faith), or better, as *scientia fidei* (*knowledge* of faith) is more apt for the work of scholasticism, while the formulation *fides quaerens intellectum* (*faith in search* of understanding) is more apt for the work of the fathers. This constant attention to the element of mystery stands out in many of the texts we have studied. It drew its nourishment from sources already mentioned: the constant reading of scripture, the inspired word of God; and the fact that patristic Christology was, by and large, the work of the Church's bishops, those charismatic (as we are coming again to appreciate) Christians whose office is to preside over the mystery of God's Church, especially in the liturgical assembly of word and sacrament. Though they were not averse to enlisting reason in the service of mystery, it was the ultimate return to mystery, especially in its scriptural and cultic verifications, which was the goal of their expositions and polemics.

But the lesson of patristic Christology for our times touches also the *content* of the dogma, especially in its supreme formulation at Chalcedon. There the Church took her definitive stance between monophysitism and Nestorianism, between, on the one hand, an exaggerated mysticism which, in its effort to assure the immanence of God's saving Word in the world, compromised both the transcendence of that Word and the integrality of the humanity which he assumed; and, on the other hand, an excess of rationalism which, in seeking to defend the two values threatened by monophysitism, compromised the immanence of the Word in our humanity. The Chalcedonian formula of one person in two distinct and integral natures was not only faithful to what God had said and done in Christ. It was also a presentation of the incarnation as the archetype of the entire Christian economy in all its elements and on every level. This important point will bear some development.

The history of Christology to our own day has witnessed that Nestorianism and monophysitism remain temptations of the human psyche, according as man is preoccupied with divine transcendence or immanence, with mystery or reason, with God's power or man's autonomy. Between the age of the fathers and the Middle Ages in the West, Spanish adoptionism (ca. 800) brought a notable recurrence of the Nestorian spirit. In the twelfth century, the *assumptus homo* Christology and the Christological nihilism of the school of Abelard brought a further threat from an extreme Antiochene Christology. (For texts and commentary on these and other later developments mentioned in this paragraph, see our study, entitled *Christ and His Mission,* Newman, 1966.) In more recent times, a strong current in Protestant (especially liberal) theology has posed the same threat in contemporary terms, as have certain positions assumed by a few Catholic theologians in recent decades.

On the other hand, the monophysite temptation has been present both in East and West, less perhaps in the form of explicit propositions than in certain one-sided devotional attitudes. Joseph Jungmann and Karl Adam, among others, have pointed out how an enduring anti-Arian reaction has brought a certain popular monophysitism, which addresses itself to Christ almost exclusively as God, and tends to neglect the mediatorial role of his humanity.

But it is not only in the sphere of Christology properly so called that Nestorianism and monophysitism as religious attitudes are enduring threats. Wherever, in the name of divine power or presence or of mystical union with the divine, Christians yield to the temptation to submerge or dissolve in the great ocean of divinity the human, the created, the temporal, the material, monophysitism as a religious attitude is present. Louis Bouyer has highlighted this (as well as the Nestorian) danger in liturgical life. The same may be said for other aspects of human life. Monophysitism is present in social and cultural Christianity whenever the hierarchical, the ecclesiastical, the supernatural, are permitted to absorb the lay, the secular, the natural, or to make these inert and passive instruments. Monophysitism is present in the spiritual life of the Christian whenever the theological virtues are, perhaps unconsciously, conceived as replacing the moral virtues. The same may be said of Nestorianism. Secularism is a Nestorianism of the social, political, economic and cultural order; and when mysticism is viewed as merely the icing on a moralistic and rationalistic cake, the interior life of the Christian has succumbed to a species of extreme Antiochenism.

But we would be wrong to conceive that all diversity in Christological affirmation points to deviation from sound doctrine and life. If the history of Christology has revealed anything, it is that there is room, within the limits set by Chalcedon, for Christological pluralism. This is the valuable witness rendered by the persevering differences between the Thomistic school, with its insistence on the unity of Christ, and the Scotistic (and Suarezian) school, with its concern for the integrality of Christ's humanity. Without excessive simplification it may be said that the role of the Thomistic school has been to witness to the values of the Alexandrian spirit, while the Scotists have kept alive whatever is valid in a moderate Antiochene (and western) Christology. Even within the Thomistic school today, the rather technical but nonetheless significant dispute on the presence or absence in Christ of a created existential principle is a further witness to the legitimacy and value of Christological pluralism. No stronger proof could be had that, even after Chalcedon, the mystery of the incarnation remains a mystery.

All of which points to the conclusion that the study of patristic Christology is today highly relevant for a balanced Christian spirit in the areas of liturgy, spirituality, apostolate, culture, and indeed the whole of life. The man who has, to some degree at least, shared the struggle of the Church fathers to express their faith in Christ with due regard for immanence and transcendence, for the unity of Christ as well as for the reality and integrality of his humanity, will have developed within himself a set of attitudes, a feel for the great Christian paradox and for the central Christian mystery, which will help him immeasurably to live and to witness to that mystery in his own life and in the world of today.

QUESTIONS FOR DISCUSSION

1. What are some of the characteristics of patristic Christology? Can you recall selections which would illustrate these characteristics?
2. How can patristic and scholastic theology be distinguished? What formulas illustrate the difference?
3. Can Nestorian and monophysite tendencies be said to be completely dead today? Explain.
4. What does patristic history teach us about Christological pluralism?

Selected Readings

Bowman, D., *The Word Made Flesh*. Englewood Cliffs: Prentice-Hall, 1963. Chapters 7-8.

Carmody, J. and Clarke, T., *Christ and His Mission*. Vol. 3 in *Sources of Christian Theology* (ed. P. Palmer). Westminster, Md.: Newman, 1966.

Grillmeier, A., *Christ in Christian Tradition, From the Apostolic Age to Chalcedon (451)*. New York: Sheed and Ward, 1965.

Hardy, E. and Richardson, C. (eds.), *Christology of the Later Fathers*. Vol. 3 in *The Library of Christian Classics*. Philadelphia: Westminster, 1954.

Kelly, J., *Early Christian Doctrines*. New York: Harper and Row, 2d ed. 1960. Chapters 6, 7, 11, 12, 14.

Mersch, E., *The Whole Christ. The Historical Development of the Doctrine of the Mystical Body in Scripture and Tradition*. Milwaukee: Bruce, 1938.

Richard, M., *The Mystery of the Redemption*. Baltimore: Helicon, 1966.

Rivière, J., *The Doctrine of the Atonement*. 2 volumes. St. Louis: B. Herder, 1909.

Sellers, R., *The Council of Chalcedon. A Historical and Doctrinal Study*. London: SPCK, 1953.

Monteau-Bonamy, H., "An Outline of the Development of Christology," in *The Historical and Mystical Christ*. Vol. 5 in *Theology Library* (ed. A. Henry). Chicago: Fides, 1958. pp. 4-35.

Index